Dea Pat & Jean

SOMETHING UNDERSTOOD

... a fett not
understood

Love,

A SPIRITUAL ANTHOLOGY

Straight
from
the
Emerald Isle

EDITED BY SEÁN DUNNE

Love,

May 1995

Other books by Seán Dunne

Poetry
Against the Storm
The Sheltered Nest

Memoir
In My Father's House

Spirituality
The Road to Silence: an Irish Spiritual Odyssey

Editor of:
Poets of Munster
An Introduction to Cork Poetry
The Cork Anthology

First published in 1995 by
Marino Books
An imprint of Mercier Press
16 Hume Street Dublin 2

Trade enquiries to Mercier Press
PO Box 5, 5 French Church Street, Cork

A Marino Original

Introduction © Seán Dunne 1995
The acknowledgements page is an
extension of this copyright notice

ISBN 1 86023 008 3

10 9 8 7 6 5 4 3 2 1

A CIP record for this title is available
from the British Library

Cover painting courtesy of the
National Gallery of Ireland
Cover design by Niamh Sharkey
Set by Richard Parfrey in Lucida Bright
8.5/11 and Avant Garde
Printed in Ireland by ColourBooks,
Baldoyle Industrial Estate, Dublin 13

CONTENTS

KINDLING THE FIRE

SOMETHING UNDERSTOOD

DOUBT AND CONVERSION

SALT OF THE EARTH

DWELLING ON LIVES

A WAY OF LIFE

GOD

PASSION AND RESURRECTION

THE FOREST OF THE DEAD

ACKNOWLEDGEMENTS

I am grateful to a number of people who helped me as I compiled this anthology. Those who helped me with texts included Father Adrian Farrelly who gave me access to the Dominican Library in Cork. Sister Miriam of the Poor Clare Convent on College Road, Cork, proved once again how her decision to become a contemp-lative allows her to take the pulse of things; I shall miss the bags of books left for me at the convent lodge. Sally Phipps made some excellent suggestions, many of which I have followed. James Roose-Evans was also very helpful with books and ideas. Father Kevin Fogarty gave me access to material held by the Cistercians at Mount Melleray Abbey in County Waterford. Phyllis Doolan introduced me to books on Francis of Assist and excerpts from these, too, have been given a space. Dermot Keogh loaned me some of his many books on South America; these reflect his ongoing interest in the story of Jean Donovan and in other political and historical aspects of that area. Reverend Gordon Pamment loaned me his lovingly thumbed *King James Bible.* Trish Edelstein, Gavin, Merlin, Niamh and Owen, yet again, patiently stepped over mounds of paper and piles of books in various corners of the house as the anthology took shape.

For permission to reprint copyright material the Publishers are grateful to the following:
The Mercier Press for the extract from *Teresa of Avila* by Kate O'Brien; Random House UK and James Sharkey Associates for the extract from *Unveiled* copyright © Mary Loudon 1992; SCM Press for extracts from Dietrich Bonhoeffer's *Letters and Papers from Prison, The Enlarged Edition* (SCM Press, 1971) and extract from chapter 3 of Leonardo Boff, *St Francis: A Model for Human Liberation,* (SCM Press, 1985); 'A Christmas Childhood' and 'Having Confessed' by kind permission of the trustees of the estate of Patrick Kavanagh, c/o Peter Fallon, Literary Agent, Loughcrew, Oldcastle, County Meath; Orbis Books for the extract from Dorothy Day's *Selected Writings* edited by Robert Ellsberg; Daphne D. C. Pochin Mould for the extract from *The Celtic Saints*; the Peters, Fraser and Dunlop Group Ltd for the extract from *Helena* by Evelyn Waugh; Stanbrook Abbey for Thomas Merton's translation of 'Guigo the Carthusian's Letter'; permission to use material from *Seeds of Contemplation* by Thomas Merton is granted by Anthony Clarke, Publishers, Wheathampstead, UK; the Marvell Press for 'Church

Going' by Philip Larkin; Brian Fallon for 'Mater Dei' by Padraic Fallon; New Island Books for 'Our Lady of Bikini' by Francis Stuart; Penguin Books Ltd for the extract from *Pensées* by Blaise Pascal, translated by A. J. Krailsheimer (Penguin Classics, 1966) copyright © A. J. Krailsheimer, the extract from *The Fire of Love* by Richard Rolle, translated by Clifton Wolters (Penguin Classics, 1972) copyright © Clifton Wolters, 1972, the extract from *The Life of St Teresa of Avila By Herself* translated by J. M. Cohen (Penguin Classics, 1957) copyright © J. M. Cohen, 1957; Cistercian publications for Hildegard of Bingen, *Scivias,* PL 197: 384. Translated by Coleman O'Dell OCSO in 'Elizabeth of Schönau and Hildegard of Bingen: Prophets of the Lord' in *Peace Weavers,* Medieval Religious Women vol. 2 ed. John A. Nichols and Lillian Thomas Shank (Kalamazoo: Cistercian Publications, 1987), p. 94; Doubleday for the extract from *Conjectures of a Guilty Bystander* by Thomas Merton; Oneworld Publications for the extract from *The Spiritual Life* by Evelyn Underhill; Eavan Boland for 'The Pilgrim' from *New Territory* copyright © Eavan Boland 1967; Salmon Publishing for 'Going to Knock' from *At This Hour of the Tide* copyright © Catherine Phil MacCarthy 1994; Sheil Land Associates Ltd for the excerpt 'Light' from *Inner Journey, Outer Journey* copyright © James Roose-Evans (Rider Books, 1987); the Paulist Press for the extract from *Francis and Clare: The Complete Works,* translated and introduced by Regis J. Armstrong OFM Cap and Ignatius Brady OFM copyright © Armstrong and Brady 1980; Cassells PLC for the extract from *John XXlll: Pope of the Council* by Peter Hebblethwaite and 'Mary of Bethany' and 'Mary of Magdala' by Margaret Hebblethwaite from *Six New Gospels: New Testament Women Tell Their Stories* copyright © Margaret Hebblethwaite 1994 published by Mowbray, London; John F. Deane for his translation of 'The Dream of the Rood'; A P Watt on behalf of the Royal Literary Fund for the extract from *Life of St Francis* by G. K. Chesterton; John McGahern for 'The Wine Breath' from *Collected Stories of John McGahern* (Faber & Faber); HarperCollins Publishers for the extract from *Catherine: Selected Writings of Catherine of Siena:* trans. Kenelm Foster and Mary John Ronayne (Collins, 1980); John Murray for 'Bells' from *English Parish Churches* copyright © John Betjeman 1958 and an extract from 'The Five Voyages of Arnor' from *Selected Poems* copyright © George Mackay Brown 1977.

Every effort has been made to contact copyright holders. The Publishers will be glad to be notified of any errors or omissions in the above list and to make good any such errors or ommissions.

INTRODUCTION

Like most Irish people, my earliest encounter with spiritual literature came through the Catholic catechism which we used in primary school. It was a small book with clear-cut questions and answers, and it was taken out of the schoolbag every day for the last class before lunchtime. On a wall above the blackboard, a statue of the Virgin Mary was perched behind glass. The truly important questions in the catechism had red dots set against them while the less important were marked by blue dots of a hue similar to the statue's cloak. I remember little of that catechism, except for a lugubrious picture of a guardian angel standing with seraphic gaze behind a child who seemed about to fall into a stream.

There was also the *Sacred Heart Messenger*, a weekly magazine which is still in print but no longer comes in the scarlet cover that marked it for decades. I once met a women who told me that she had used the cover of the *Sacred Heart Messenger* to rouge her cheeks before a dance. It was one of a number of magazines and newspapers that contained short religious articles and instructive snippets: *The Far East, The Word, The Universe, The Catholic Standard, The Irish Catholic*. Saint Martin de Porres had a magazine to himself, as did Saint Anthony. *The Word*, in particular, was very good since it made excellent use of photographs and also contained articles that were of more than passing interest, even to a child. It avoided the pious air that dominated so many of the others.

Outside these again, there were the publications of the Catholic Truth Society. These seemed to run into the thousands. Their opening pages contained important-looking Latin words like *Imprimatur* and *Nihil Obstat*. These pamphlets lay in dark wooden racks on walls at the backs of churches and covered a wide range of topics. I liked to peruse them, just as I liked to peruse anything with words on it, but the only ones that I recall now are those which dealt with sex and puberty. I read them with lascivious curiosity in early adolescence. I had no interest in any moral message that they might have imparted: rather, I was looking for sexual details. The Catholic Truth Society pamphlets proved quite unsatisfactory in this regard.

The *Sacred Heart Messenger* and other publications were part of the landscape of childhood, as natural a part of the surroundings as Milk of Magnesia or boxes of Lego bricks. Each Sunday, *The Universe* came through the letterbox. It was scanned rather than read, but its presence was enough. Like the *Daily Telegraph* or *Pravda*, it stood for a code and merely having it in your house declared your allegiance to what it represented.

As a glance through any collection of old copies will show, the quality of writing in such publications was generally poor. It still is: in the case of Irish Catholicism especially, the lack of a well written journal or magazine has been a reflection of the gap that is sometimes felt between a childhood allegiance to a particular faith and the grown-up, questioning self. Intellectuals and the Catholic Church in Ireland have been wary of each other; there has been no equivalent of C. S. Lewis, say, or of a great magazine like *The Tablet*. Good publications such as *Intercom* and *The Furrow* tend to be pitched at a clerical readership. A grown-up faith demands grown-up writing, but in the twentieth century many of the writers moved away or were condemned, or simply had no interest in writing on religious matters. Efforts to right this, such as the meetings of the Common Ground society in Dublin in the 1940's, foundered in time. Those who attended the meetings of Common Ground included the writers Peadar O'Donnell, Sean O'Faolain and Patrick Kavanagh (a poet who once worked as film critic with the *Catholic Standard*, a post in which he was succeeded by another poet, John Montague) and the founder of the Legion of Mary, Frank Duff. Ireland has a very poor library of religious literature. Despite the fact that the Irish language contains a rich religious literature, good religious literature in Ireland amounts to no more than a tit's egg when compared with England or France.

This gap became more apparent to me as I compiled this anthology. The idea that religion can be written about with as much care as any other subject is sadly foreign to many writers and to many Irish journalists in particular. In journalism, there have been exceptions – Andy Pollak and Louis MacRedmond, for example – but, too often, religious debate is polarised between those for whom religion is an absurdity from their own childhood and those for whom it is a cause of fundamentalist fervour. The articles that attack the ideal of religion (popular Sunday newspapers are a particularly predictable forum for these) are often written from a dated agenda that is as tired as its opposite (which finds a home, say, in the *Irish Catholic*). A kind of oedipal frenzy faces a fundamentalist piety. Often this polarisation is a reflection of personal prejudices rather than of intelligent reflection. If I know this, it is only because I once inhabited the anti-religious side of this debate myself.

One only has to read a few pages from Newman to see the manner in which religion can be written about with style and intellect. His work is a classic conjunction of faith and intelligence. Likewise, the subtleties which fiction-writers and poets have displayed when taking religion as a theme have reached a depth that journalistic coverage can never attain. It is not, of course, that one would expect to have a world of Newmans and McGaherns (while John McGahern has told interviewers that he is not a practising Catholic, his stories, like those of other Irish writers, are often accurate depictions of a Catholic world); rather, such writers affirm the fact that religion can be written about in a way that does honour to words and does not treat them as agents of pap or propaganda. Thus, some of the finest references to the spirituality of Saint Thérèse of Lisieux can be found in the novels of Francis Stuart rather than in some hagiographical pamphlet. Likewise, the poems of Patrick Kavanagh contain an extraordinary spirituality. His poem 'Having Confessed' is among the most humble I know.

Such work as Kavanagh's comes from the core of faith, an area that exists in a space removed from that arena of scandal, brutality and authoritarianism which provides newspapers with so much subject matter. Churches and scandal have gone together through the ages but this inner core remains unscathed. Gibbon's history of ancient Rome tells of splits and rows between the earliest Christians; any decent book on the middle ages will have its share of things rotten in the state of Rome.

For spirituality touches the deepest aspects of existence. It is surprising, then, that it has probably engendered more bad writing than any other area of human interest. The spirituality sections of most bookshops are filled with books that display a mediocre style masked as meaningful reflection. The trite and the sentimental vie for space with the vapid and the self-indulgent. The meaningful is too often the unreadable. The mere mention of God seems enough for such books and pamphlets to get into print. Often they may even be written in the form of poems: vapid, airy thoughts broken into lines that look like the lines of poems but read like a parody of all that makes poetry worthwhile. Even a minor religious work by a great writer – Evelyn Waugh's *Helena* for example – seems, by comparison, the product of genius.

Others dispense with mock-poetry and opt for a heavy prose that aims for theological seriousness and makes no pretence at literary worth. Here, nobody from the latest Dutch theologian to the Pope is immune. As a common reader with an interest in such matters, I have found most of these books impossible to read and have felt only sympathy for those seminarians or fundamentalists (I can think of no other who might want to read them in full) who must study them as set texts.

This is a shame, because surely God is as well served by a beautifully honed sentence as by a carefully composed liturgy, a finely carved altar or a Gregorian chant. Creative writers, who are often intellectuals who scoff at religion, have of late tended not to get involved in religious matters. In Ireland especially, there have been very few prose writers in whom religious belief has combined with literary worth.

To some extent, the poor quality of spiritual writing is understandable. Through the sixties and seventies, religion was not fashionable among intellectuals. It was easier to quote Graham Greene than live within a faith that, in a world that grows less dependent on religion, seems on a par with witch-doctors and mediums. The world has moved on from being a place where thousands of homes had holy-water founts inside the front door. Now, such founts might feature in colour supplement features as examples of a craze for kitsch in interior design. Those artists who have taken religious themes for their work – Patrick Pye, for example, or Ken Thompson – have ploughed a marginal furrow. While discussing the work of an artist whose themes have a religious basis, I was asked by an art student: 'Yes, I know his work but isn't he some kind of religious nut?'

There is another problem which confronts the editor of a spiritual anthology. At its most intense, spiritual experience is wordless and, at the very most (as the medieval writer of 'The Cloud of Unknowing' tells us), may need no more than a single word to express its own depth. At the height of meditation, mystics enter into the realm of silence rather than the realm of words, and to communicate that experience in words must seem impossible. If Wittgenstein could declare: 'The limits of my language are the limits of my world,' those who know religion as an interior experience could likewise declare: 'The limits of my world are declared by the limits of my silence.' In the beginning was the word; in the end is silence. The contemplative and prayerful element is a feature of this book; inadequate as such fragments might be, they are still correlatives for the sermon of silence, an experience that touches the core of belief.

A few have managed to convey this experience with particular brilliance. Teresa of Avila, for example, had a genius for expression that matched her genius for holiness. The same is true of John Henry Newman and Dietrich Bonhoeffer. Yet in compiling an anthology of spiritual writings, I was not simply guided by the need to combine a selection of pieces that, where possible, had literary worth. I was also guided, as in the case of these writers, by the need to communicate aspects of spirituality in a way that is real and true, and that is free of the kind of piety that prefers to think of saints as rose-bordered visions rather than as people who, among their more spectacular and troubled achievements, shaved or sewed or walked through plain streets where rain or sunlight fell. As Patrick Kavanagh realised, it is in the way that it can imbue the everyday that spirituality is at its most potent. Thérèse of Lisieux encapsulated this concept in her theory of the little way, whereby full and loving attention was given to whatever task is at hand, no matter how humble. For Teresa of Avila, God moved among the pots and pans while others heard Him among the church-bells, or sensed His presence among the changing seasons or, like Dorothy Day, among workers or the poor.

I also wanted to gather a store of writings that would transmit aspects of religious experience in a way that would make them real for an age that is growing increasingly uninterested in religion even as it hungers for spiritual answers. We have moved from a period of certainty to a period of doubt, search and lack of interest. The search can be a rich one, as many of the writers represented in this book attest. It is no accident that the section on doubt and conversion has more pieces than any other, since doubt is now as common as dust. The search which others have made may be a reflection of one's own journey. It may also be, as has been the case with Saint Augustine for centuries, a reflection of a situation in which many people find themselves as they live out the exigencies of an ordinary life.

Although not specifically requested by my publisher to do so, I have compiled an anthology which draws entirely on the Christian tradition, and which in turn draws richly from the Catholic expression of that tradition. My reason for this is simple. For many years, I read and wandered through other faiths before returning, like Odysseus, to the point from which I had set out. Like many others, I felt a need for spiritual answers. I sensed aspects of this search in places, situations and books – at the church of Saint

Gervais, in Paris, for example, or in certain passages from the writings of Thomas Merton. In Quakerism, I discovered the fruitful link between silence and spirituality. In Buddhism, I encountered an enriching stress on the nature of change and also an emphasis on the importance of meditation. The Amish and the Shakers made me notice the way in which objects – a quilt, a cake, a poem – can contain a quality that reflects the spiritual life of the maker. Such emphases led me down many by-roads but, ultimately, I was never quite comfortable enough to settle on any particular one.

It was only when I began to explore the Christian tradition in some depth that I discovered many of these same elements. They had been buried by the narrow image of the Church that I had partly inherited and partly created. More and more people are rediscovering them now. The Christian tradition, growing for almost two thousand years, has extraordinary riches that include the door of Notre Dame cathedral and stories of the Desert Fathers. This anthology is a reflection of my own reading in this area; its limitations are my own and not the tradition's. Were I to include fragments of other traditions, I would not be serving them in a proper manner and they would seem inadequately represented.

I discovered, too, the *world* of Christianity and not merely an island on the edge of Europe. The writings of medieval English mystics such as Julian of Norwich, Richard Rolle and the author of 'The Cloud of Unknowing' mean as much to me now as the nature poems of early Irish monks or the great Celtic prayers with which the *Carmina Gadelica* is filled. Thomas Merton, standing in reflection at an American street-corner or campaigning against the spread of war, is closer to me than most writers. Simone Weil's intense reflections as she 'waited on God' are part of the climate of our time, while Margaret Hebblethwaite's recreations of the women who knew Jesus are part of an enriching communication that broadens and deepens belief. Dietrich Bonhoeffer, writing from his cell in Germany, is somehow more central to our age than a comfortable cardinal writing from an office where, in the words of a South American poet, 'faith lies filed in folders.'

Behind much of this selection lies a particular shadow. It belongs to a woman named Jean Donovan who was raped and murdered in El Salvador in 1980. A few years before, she had been a student in University College, Cork, when I myself was a student there. It was only when I saw her photograph in *Time* magazine in the weeks after her death that I recognised, with horror, the woman whom I

had seen around college, distinctive in a check jacket and a cap.
Jean Donovan grew up in an American family that was typical of
its culture. She was no wilting pietist; she understood politics and
economics, and she understood, too, that American involvement in
El Salvador was, in the truest sense, a sin. She had come back from
El Salvador to Cork and some of her friends had pleaded with her
not to return. There had been warnings and threats: priests and
nuns had been killed, missionaries had been attacked. Yet she had
to go back, she said, especially for the children; to stay away would
be to abandon them. She knew that if one side of religious
experience has to do with prayer and contemplation, then the other
side has to do with how we treat others, and that one without the
other is like a song without a singer. In this way, religious belief is
both solitary and relational.

Jean Donovan went back to El Salvador and, with a group of
Maryknoll missionaries, she was killed. Later, her family – up to
then a typical family in Ronald Reagan's America – grew so
frustrated trying to discover the truth behind her death that they
would bring their children with them when going to the State
Department in Washington. It would be harder, they thought, for
officials to tell lies in front of children.

Jean Donovan's story affected me deeply. I had thought of
martyrs as technicolour illustrations in some of those little
magazines that I knew as a child. They belonged to another age.
Jean Donovan brought home to me the fact that religious belief is
not a comfortable sofa for the mind. Neither is it a dated
superstition for the ignorant. It is paramount as an inner experience
and also as social attitude in a world where the Crucifixion is an
accurate image of life for a great many people. Despite the emphasis
of our age, we cannot be perfect. To be human is also to be broken
in some way, but our very brokenness is also part of that which
heals. It involves a praxis between belief and action and, as Jean
Donovan showed, it can take one to extremes that can even cause
one's death. In a world of screaming stock exchanges, of clinical
wars and casual indifference to the pain of others, her example
remains a challenge to many elements of contemporary experience.
This book, with its fragments from many sources, is dedicated to
her memory, and it is also dedicated to her friend Máire Corkery,
who remains one of my own sustaining friends.

Seán Dunne
Cork, February 1995

GEORGE BERNANOS

STAR AND HEART

From the beginning, My Church has been what it is today, and will be until the end of time, a scandal to the strong, a disappointment to the weak, the ordeal and the consolation of those interior souls who seek in it nothing but Myself. Yes . . . whoever looks for Me there will find Me there; but he will have to look, and I am better hidden than people think, or than certain of My priests would have you believe. I am still more difficult to discover than I was in the little stable at Bethlehem for those who will not approach Me humbly, in the footsteps of the shepherds and the Magi. It is true that palaces have been built in My honor, with galleries and peristyles without number, magnificently illuminated day and night, populated with guards and sentries. But if you want to find Me there, the clever thing is to do as they did on the old road in Judaea, buried under the snow, and ask for the only thing you need – a star and a pure heart.

DIETRICH BONHOEFFER

LETTER FROM PRISON

TO HIS PARENTS 17 DECEMBER 1943

There's probably nothing for it but to write you a Christmas letter now to meet all eventualities. Although it passes my comprehension that they may possibly still keep me here over Christmas, I've learnt in the past eight and a half months that the unexpected often happens, and that what can't be changed must be accepted with a *sacrificium intellectus*, although the *sacrificium* is not quite complete, and the *intellectus* silently goes its own way.

Above all, you mustn't think that I'm going to let myself be depressed by this lonely Christmas; it will always take its special place among the other unusual Christmases that I've kept in Spain, America, and England, and I want in later years to look back on the time here, not with shame, but with a certain pride. That's the only thing that no one can take from me.

Of course, you, Maria and the family and friends, can't help thinking of my being in prison over Christmas, and it's bound to cast a shadow over the few happy hours that are left to you in these times. The only thing I can do to help is to believe and know that your thoughts about it will be the same as mine, and that we shall be at one in our attitude towards the keeping of this Christmas. Indeed, it can't be otherwise, for that attitude is simply a spiritual inheritance from you. I needn't tell you how I long to be released and to see you all again. But for years you have given us such perfectly lovely Christmases that our grateful recollection of them is strong enough to put a darker one into the background. It's not till such times as these that we realise what it means to possess a past and a spiritual inheritance independent of changes of time and circumstance. The consciousness of being borne up by a spiritual tradition that goes back for centuries gives one a feeling of confidence and security in the face of all passing strains and stresses. I believe that anyone who is aware of such reserves of strength needn't be ashamed of more tender feelings evoked by the memory of a rich and noble past, for in my opinion they belong to the better and nobler part of mankind. They will not overwhelm those who hold fast to values that no one can take from them.

From the Christian point of view there is no special problem about Christmas in a prison cell. For many people in this building it will probably be a more sincere and genuine occasion than in places where nothing but the name is kept. That misery, suffering, poverty, loneliness, helplessness, and guilt mean something quite different in the eyes of God from what they mean in the judgment of man, that God will approach where men turn away, that Christ was born in a stable because there was no room for him in the inn – these are things that a prisoner can understand better than other people; for him they really are glad tidings, and that faith gives him a part in the communion of saints, a Christian fellowship breaking the bounds of time and space and reducing the months of confinement here to insignificance . . .

ANONYMOUS

THE VIRGIN AND CHILD

On yesternight I saw a sight,
    A star as bright as day;
And all along I heard a song,
    Lullay, by by, lullay.

A lovely Lady sat and sang,
    And to her Child she spake;
'My Son, my Brother, Father dear,
    It makes my heart to ache
        To see Thee there
        So cold and bare,
    A King upon this hay;
        But hush Thy wail,
        I will not fail
    To sing by by, lullay.'

The Child then spake whilst she did sing,
    And to the Maiden said,
'Right sure I am a mighty King,
    Though is a crib My bed;
        For Angels bright
        Down to Me light;
    Thou canst not say Me nay;
        Then why so sad?
        Thou mayst be glad
    To sing by by, lullay.'

'Now, sweetest Lord, since Thou art King,
    Why liest Thou in a stall?
Why didst Thou not Thy cradle bring
    To some great royal hall?
        Methinks 'tis right
        That king or knight
    Should lie in good array;
        And them among
        It were no wrong
    To sing by by, lullay.'

'My Mother Mary, thine I be,
    Though I be laid in stall,
Both lords and dukes shall worship Me,
    And so shall monarchs all:
        Ye shall well see
        That Princes Three
    Shall come on the twelfth day.
        Then let Me rest
        Upon thy breast
    And sing by by, lullay.'

'Now tell me, sweetest Lord, I pray,
    Thou art my Love and Dear,
How shall I nurse Thee to Thy mind,
    And make Thee glad of cheer?
        For all Thy will
        I would fulfil,
    I need no more to say;
        And for all this
        I will Thee kiss,
    And sing by by, lullay.'

'My Mother dear, when time it be,
    Then take Me up aloft,
And set Me up upon thy knee,
    And handle Me full soft;
        And in thy arm
        Thou wilt Me warm,
    And keep Me night and day:

And if I weep,
    And may not sleep,
Thou sing by by, lullay.'

'Now, sweetest Lord, since it is so,
    That Thou art most of might,
I pray Thee grant a boon to me,
    If it be meet and right;
        That child or man
        That will or can
    Be merry on this day;
        To bliss them bring,
        And I shall sing,
    Lullay, by by, Lullay.'

PATRICK KAVANAGH

A CHRISTMAS CHILDHOOD

1

One side of the potato-pits was white with frost –
How wonderful that was, how wonderful!
And when we put our ears to the paling-post
The music that came out was magical.

The light between the ricks of hay and straw
Was a hole in Heaven's gable. An apple tree
With its December-glinting fruit we saw –
O you, Eve, were the world that tempted me

To eat the knowledge that grew in clay
And death the germ within it! Now and then
I can remember something of the gay
Garden that was childhood's. Again

The tracks of cattle to a drinking-place,
A green stone lying sideways in a ditch
Or any common sight the transfigured face
Of a beauty that the world did not touch.

II

My father played the melodeon
Outside at our gate;
There were stars in the morning east
And they danced to his music.

Across the wild bogs his melodeon called
To Lennons and Callans.
As I pulled on my trousers in a hurry
I knew some strange thing had happened.

Outside in the cow-house my mother
Made the music of milking;
The light of her stable-lamp was a star
And the frost of Bethlehem made it twinkle.

A water-hen screeched in the bog,
Mass-going feet
Crunched the wafer-ice on the pot-holes,
Somebody wistfully twisted the bellows wheel.

My child poet picked out the letters
On the grey stone,
In silver the wonder of a Christmas townland,
The winking glitter of a frosty dawn.

Cassiopeia was over
Cassidy's hanging hill,
I looked and three whin bushes rode across
The horizon – the Three Wise Kings.

An old man passing said:
'Can't he make it talk' –
The melodeon. I hid in the doorway
And tightened the belt of my box-pleated coat.

I nicked six nicks on the door-post
With my penknife's big blade –
There was a little one for cutting tobacco.
And I was six Christmases of age.

My father played the melodeon,
My mother milked the cows,
And I had a prayer like a white rose pinned
On the Virgin Mary's blouse.

EVELYN WAUGH

EPIPHANY

But by Twelfth Night she rallied and on the eve set out by litter along the five rough miles to the shrine of the Nativity. There was no throng of pilgrims. Macarius and his people kept Epiphany in their own church. Only the little community of Bethlehem greeted her and led her to the room they had prepared. She rested there dozing until an hour before dawn when they called her and led her out under the stars, then down into the stable-cave, where they made a place for her on the women's side of the small, packed congregation.

The low vault was full of lamps and the air close and still. Silver bells announced the coming of the three vested, bearded monks, who like the kings of old now prostrated themselves before the altar. So the long liturgy began.

Helena knew little Greek and her thoughts were not in the words nor anywhere in the immediate scene. She forgot even her quest and was dead to everything except the swaddled child long ago and those three royal sages who had come from so far to adore him.

'This is my day,' she thought, 'and these are my kind.'

Perhaps she apprehended that her fame, like theirs, would live in one historic act of devotion; that she too had emerged from a kind of $ov'\tau o\pi \acute{\iota}\alpha$ or nameless realm and would vanish like them in the sinking nursery fire-light among the picturebooks and the day's toys.

'Like me,' she said to them, 'you were late in coming. The shepherds were here long before; even the cattle. They had joined the chorus of angels before you were on your way. For you the primordial discipline of the heavens was relaxed and a new defiant light blazed amid the disconcerted stars.

'How laboriously you came, taking sights and calculating, where the shepherds had run barefoot! How odd you looked on the road, attended by what outlandish liveries, laden with such preposterous gifts!

'You came at length to the final stage of your pilgrimage and the great star stood still above you. What did you do? You stopped to call on King Herod. Deadly exchange of compliments in which began that unended war of mobs and magistrates against the innocent!

'Yet you came, and were not turned away. You too found room before the manger. Your gifts were not needed, but they were accepted and put carefully by, for they were brought with love. In that new order of charity that had just come to life, there was room for you, too. You were not lower in the eyes of the holy family than the ox or the ass.

'You are my especial patrons,' said Helena, 'and patrons of all late-comers, of all who have a tedious journey to make to the truth, of all who are confused with knowledge and speculation, of all who through politeness make themselves partners in guilt, of all who stand in danger by reason of their talents.

'Dear cousins, pray for me,' said Helena, 'and for my poor overloaded son. May he, too, before the end find kneeling-space in the straw. Pray for the great, lest they perish utterly. And pray for Lactantius and Marcias and the young poets of Trèves and for the souls of my wild, blind ancestors; for their sly foe Odysseus and for the great Longinus.

'For His sake who did not reject your curious gifts, pray always for all the learned, the oblique, the delicate. Let them not be quite forgotten at the Throne of God when the simple come into their kingdom.'

ANONYMOUS

THE BITTER WITHY

As it fell out upon a bright holiday,
Small hail from the sky did fall.
Our Saviour asked his mother mild,
'Can I go out and play at the ball?'

'At the ball, the ball, my own dear son
It's time that you was gone;
But it's don't let me hear of any mischief
At night when you come home.'

So it's up the hill and it's down the hill
Our sweet young Saviour ran,
Until he come to three rich lords' sons:
'Good morning, sirs, each one.'

'Good morn, good morn, and good morn,' says they;
'It's thrice good morn,' says he,
'And it's which of you three rich lords' sons
Is gonna play at the ball with me?'

'Why we, we're lords', we're ladies' sons
Born in a bower or hall.
But you, you're nothing but a poor maid's child,
You was born in an ox's stall.'

'Well, if I'm nothing but a poor maid's child
Born in an ox's stall,
I'll make you believe in your latter end
That I'm an angel above you all.'

And so he build him a bridge with the rays of the sun.
Over the river ran he.
Them three rich lords' sons, they followed him,
And it's drowned they were, all three.

And it's up the hill and it's down the hill
Three weeping mothers ran
Saying, 'Mary mild, take home your child,
For ours he's drowned, each one.'

And so it's Mary Mild, she took home her child,
She laid him across her knee,
And it's with a switch of the bitter withy
She's given him slashes three.

'Oh bitter withy, oh bitter withy,
You caused me to smart;
And now the willow shall be the very first tree
Gonna perish at the heart.'

THE DEAREST FRESHNESS

GERARD MANLEY HOPKINS

GOD'S GRANDEUR

The world is charged with the grandeur of God.
It will flame out, like shining from shook foil;
It gathers to a greatness, like the ooze of oil
Crushed. Why do men then now not reck his rod?
Generations have trod, have trod, have trod;
And all is seared with trade; bleared, smeared with toil;
And wears man's smudge and shares man's smell: the soil
Is bare now, nor can foot feel, being shod.

And for all this, nature is never spent;
There lives the dearest freshness deep down things;
And though the last lights off the black West went
Oh, morning, at the brown brink eastward, springs -
Because the Holy Ghost over the bent
World broods with warm breast and with ah! bright wings.

HENRY DAVID THOREAU

SOLITUDE

One of the crowded hives of Cambridge College is as solitary as a
dervish in the desert. The farmer can work alone in the field or the
woods all day, hoeing or chopping, and not feel lonesome, because
he is employed; but when he comes home at night he cannot sit
down in a room alone, at the mercy of his thoughts, but must be

where he can 'see the folks', and recreate, and, as he thinks, remunerate himself for his day's solitude; and hence he wonders how the student can sit alone in the house all night and most of the day without ennui and 'the blues'; but he does not realise that the student, though in the house, is still at work in *his* field, and chopping in *his* woods, as the farmer in his, and in turn seeks the same recreation and society that the latter does, though it may be a more condensed form of it.

Society is commonly too cheap. We meet at very short intervals, not having had time to acquire any new value for each other. We meet at meals three times a-day, and give each other a new taste of that old musty cheese that we are. We have had to agree on a certain set of rules, called etiquette and politeness, to make this frequent meeting tolerable and that we need not come to open war. We meet at the post office, and at the sociable, and about the fireside every night; we live thick and are in each other's way, and stumble over one another, and I think that we thus lose some respect for one another. Certainly less frequency would suffice for all important and hearty communications. Consider the girls in a factory, – never alone, hardly in their dreams. It would be better if there were but one inhabitant to a square mile, as where I live. The value of a man is not in his skin, that we should touch him.

I have heard of a man lost in the woods and dying of famine and exhaustion at the foot of a tree, whose loneliness was relieved by the grotesque visions with which, owing to bodily weakness, his diseased imagination surrounded him, and which he believed to be real. So also, owing to bodily and mental health and strength, we may be continually cheered by a like but more normal and natural society, and come to know that we are never alone.

I have a great deal of company in my house; especially in the morning, when nobody calls. Let me suggest a few comparisons, that some one may convey an idea of my situation. I am no more lonely than the loon in the pond that laughs so loud, or than Walden Pond itself. What company has that lonely lake, I pray? And yet it has not the blue devils, but the blue angels in it, in the azure tint of its waters. The sun is alone, except in thick weather, when there sometimes appear to be two, but one is a mock sun. God is alone, – but the devil, he is far from being alone; he sees a great deal of company; he is legion. I am no more lonely than a single mullein or dandelion in a pasture, or a bean leaf, or sorrel, or a horse-fly, or a humble bee. I am no more lonely than the Mill Brook, or a weathercock, or the north star, or the south wind, or an April shower, or a January thaw, or the first spider in a new house.

I have occasional visits in the long winter evenings, when the snow falls fast and the wind howls in the wood, from an old settler and original proprietor, who is reported to have dug Walden Pond, and stoned it, and fringed it with pine woods: who tells me stories of old time and of new eternity; and between us we manage to pass a cheerful evening with social mirth and pleasant views of things, even without apples or cider, – a most wise and humorous friend, whom I love much, who keeps himself more secret than ever did Goffe of Whalley; and though he is thought to be dead, none can show where he is buried. An elderly dame, too, dwells in my neighbourhood, invisible to most persons, in whose odorous herb garden I love to stroll sometimes, gathering simples and listening to her fables; for she has a genius of unequalled fertility, and her memory runs back farther than mythology, and she can tell me the original of every fable, and on what fact every one is founded, for the incidents occurred when she was young. A ruddy and lusty old dame, who delights in all weathers and seasons, and is likely to outlive all her children yet.

The indescribable innocence and beneficence of Nature, – of sun, and wind, and rain, of summer and winter, – such health, such cheer, they afford for ever! and such sympathy have they ever with our race, that all Nature would be affected, and the sun's brightness fade, and the winds would sigh humanely, and the clouds rain tears, and the woods shed their leaves and put on mourning in midsummer, if any man should ever for a just cause grieve. Shall I not have intelligence with the earth? Am I not partly leaves and vegetable mould myself?

What is the pill which will keep us well, serene, contented? Not my or thy great-grandfather's, but our great-grandmother Nature's universal, vegetable, botanic medicines, by which she has kept herself young always, outlived so many old Parrs in her day, and fed her health with their decaying fatness. For my panacea, instead of one of those quack vials of a mixture dipped from Acheron and the Dead Sea, which come out of those long shallow black-schooner-looking waggons which we sometimes see made to carry bottles, let me have a draught of undiluted morning air. Morning air! If men will not drink of this at the fountain-head of the day, why, then, we must even bottle up some and sell it in the shops, for the benefit of those who have lost their subscription ticket to morning time in this world. But remember, it will not keep quite till noonday even in the coolest cellar, but drive out the stopples long ere that and follow westward the steps of Aurora. I am no worshipper of Hygeia, who was the daughter of that old herb-doctor Æsculapius, and who is represented on monuments holding a serpent in one hand, and in the other a cup out of which the serpent sometimes drinks; but rather of Hebe, cup-bearer to Jupiter, who was the daughter of Juno and wild lettuce, and who had the power of restoring gods and men to the vigour of youth. She was probably the only thoroughly sound-conditioned, healthy, and robust young lady that ever walked the globe, and whenever she came it was spring.

DAPHNE D. C. POCHIN MOULD

THE EARTH IS THE LORD'S

Pagan Ireland already had a love of nature and many folklore stories about animals; with this ancient tradition the new Christian one mingled, and blossomed forth in the immense animal literature about the Celtic saints. Much of it is inevitably pure romance and miracle, but the basis is in the reality of the Celtic saints' love for all creation and delight in the diversity of animal and plant.

Just as Martin could halt the dogs, so the traditions tell of the Celtic saints keeping herds within certain bounds that they marked out for them with their croziers, so that they should not stray. St Columbanus is said to have been worried by a bear robbing his orchard, he, like St Anthony in the desert, interviewed the bear and told it that it could have certain trees for its own use and must leave the rest alone for the monks.

There are many stories about bees, for honey was an important foodstuff. One beautiful little story tells how a priest lost the Host whilst carrying it on a journey and the bees found it. They set to work and made a tabernacle and church and model priests all in wax, and placed the Host there for safety. Meantime, the priest was very distressed and did penance for a year, at the end of which he was brought to the bees' wax church and recovered the Host.

St Patrick is said, when he began to build his new church at

Armagh, to have found a deer and its fawn on the site. The men with him wanted to kill it, but Patrick would not allow this and took up the fawn in his arms and carried it off to another hill nearby where it could be left in safety.

The list could be continued almost indefinitely, from wonder stories like that of the bees and the Host, to probabilities like Patrick and the fawn. But they all lead back to this basic attitude of the Celtic saints to animals and nature, and the use of their interest and delightfulness and beauty as a kind of ladder leading up toward God. The mind does not rest in created things, but looks beyond them and breaks out into praise of their Creator. Columcille in the *Altus Prosator* brought out this point in his description of the creation. He tells of God making heaven and earth, sea and waters, the blades of grass, the twigs of shrubs, the sun and the moon and the stars, the birds and the fish and the cattle, and finally, man himself. As soon as the stars were made, Columcille says the angels broke out in praise of God for the wonder of His creation. That idea, of course, continues in the *Benedicite, omnia opera Domini Domino* of the three children in the fiery furnace, the whole of creation being called upon to praise the God Who made them. That canticle, which is included in the Antiphonary of Bangor, must have been kept well to the fore in the people's minds by the very frequency of the carvings of the children on the high crosses.

But there was probably a deeper level in this love of nature of the Celtic Church. Nobody can sing the psalms or read the Bible without to some extent appreciating their references to natural beauty, to mountain and spring and torrent, but equally, one can be led to a sense of their symbolism of other spiritual realities. The Celtic saint, who had so often herded cattle in his youth, would so very readily pass from the watching of the sheep stringing out over the Irish hillside, to the scriptural symbols, the good shepherd leading out his flock onto the mountain pastures and letting them drink at the fountain of living water – the grace of the Holy Ghost. And if he, like Patrick on Croagh Patrick or Brendan on Mount Brandon or Assicus on Slieve League, built himself a hermitage on the top of a mountain, he would not only appreciate the ever-changing pattern of sea and mountain and field set out below him, but would also be constantly brought back to the scriptural symbolism of mountains.

For the hermit on the heights, when the mist swept down upon the tops, he could not but be reminded of the cloud on Sinai and Moses, or of the Transfiguration of Christ. Christ Himself had gone off up the mountain to pray, and the Celtic saints followed in His track, realising, as they did so, that His action meant more than a mere hill climb, that it symbolised the need of every Christian to go apart and pray in the solitude of the high places.

The mountain symbol is interwoven through the scriptures, and the Celtic saints would be quick to catch the different meanings: the mountain standing for Christ, or for the Church, or for preachers, and so on. The picture in Psalm 103, of the Lord sending rain upon the hills, would bring them at once to the idea of Christian teachers and preachers raised up like mountains and receiving the rain of wisdom to pass on to the lowlands of ordinary people. Or again, they might think of the mountain symbolising Christ Himself in the clean beauty of the rocky heights, the summit from which all the meaning and pattern of the world below can be discovered.

Yet again, there is the constant idea of the spiritual life as an ascent, from the valley of humility up to God. We are back with Moses on Sinai, we scramble up the heights of prayer as best we can and God stoops down from heaven to meet us, as it were, half-way.

There were deer running wild on the Irish hills in the period of the Celtic Church, just as they run wild on the Scottish mountains today, stepping elegantly over the grass and springing easily amongst the rocks and across the streams. The stag, its hooves clattering on the bare rock as it passed the Celtic hermitage, might well bring to mind another aspect of the mountain symbol – the deer as standing for the Christian, moving in nimble bounds up to the heights of contemplation (Psalm 17 uses this symbolism, v.34, where God is said to have made the singer's feet like those of the deer and brought him out onto the heights). As the stag moves off the rock and lowers its head to crop the grass in the corry, the Celtic saints may have thought of the Christian feeding on the teachings of the apostles and preachers that the mountains symbolise and from them gaining strength to go bounding over the summit ridges.

Certainly, Celtic Ireland knew the deer well, and the stories of the saints tell of their friendship with them – the tame doe that milks herself into a stone basin for the benefit of one of the saints being a recurrent hagiographical theme.

There is another aspect to the symbolism of the mountain and to the Celtic hermitages on the heights: there is a price to be paid for the freedom of the hills, the ascent has a penitential side to it. There is a renunciation of the comfortable things of this world, the snugness of the glen and the fireside, the shelter of the wood and the ease of smooth walking, for the rock and the sting of wind-driven hail – and the splendour of the beauty of the summits. It is the paradox of Christianity that you must, as it were, abandon and leave behind the lowlands of this world in order to climb out onto the heights, but when you have gained the ridge, the country beneath can be seen, and enjoyed, for what is really is, for the first time. And this is perhaps the key to the attitude of the Celtic saints to nature, the man on the mountain top, joined to God in the cloud of contemplation, but yet able to look back, down the sudden drop of the precipice and the smooth grassy slopes of the hillside, to the world beneath, the sparkling sea, the sand of the beaches, the checker-board of little fields, the dark gashes of the peat cuttings, the smoke rising from the cottage chimneys, and take delight in all these things without becoming lost and mazed amongst them. The man on the low ground may be confused and bewildered, even lost, amongst the trees or the bogs or the fields; the mountaineer is seeing the whole of the picture.

GERARD MANLEY HOPKINS

SPRING

Nothing is so beautiful as Spring –
When weeds, in wheels, shoot long and lovely and lush;
Thrush's eggs look little low heavens, and thrush
Through the echoing timber does so rinse and wring
The ear, it strikes like lightnings to hear him sing;
The glassy peartree leaves and blooms, they brush
The descending blue; that blue is all in a rush
With richness; the racing lambs too have fair their fling.

What is all this juice and all this joy?
A strain of the earth's sweet being in the beginning
In Eden garden. – Have, get, before it cloy,
Before it cloud, Christ, lord, and sour with sinning,
Innocent mind and Mayday in girl and boy,
Most, O maid's child, thy choice and worthy the winning.

DOROTHY DAY

NEW LIFE

I

October 1925: Every year the beaches around New York change, but
so gradually, one notices the changes only year by year. The
shoreline down by our little house is irregular, with many little bays
and creeks wandering inland every few miles. Some years before, a
pier a quarter of a mile down the beach toward the open ocean fell
to ruin in a storm, with the result that the sand is washed away
from our beach to be piled up on the next one . . .

The seagulls scream over the rocks, blue and gray and dazzling
white, winging their way from the wreck of the old excursion boat
to the larger rocks in the water, diving with a splash into the shallow
gray water for a fish. The waves, the gulls, and the cawing of the

crows in the woods in back of the house are the only sounds on these fall days.

Farther up and down the beach, away from our tiny bay, the waves roll in from the ocean, crashing dull and ominous on the sands, but here by the house, except during storms, the waves are gentle and playful.

I wander every afternoon up and down the beach for miles, collecting mussels, garlanded in seaweed, torn loose from the piers – pockets full of jingle shells which look as though they are made of mother of pearl and gunmetal. When the tide goes out these little cups of shells are left along the beach, each holding a few drops of water which serve to glorify both the shape and coloring of the shell.

The little house I have furnished very simply with a driftwood stove in one corner, plenty of books, comfortable chairs and couches, and my writing table in the window where I can look out at the water all day.

* * *

Late this afternoon the wind dropped and I sat by the open door contemplating the sunset. The waves lapped the shore, tingling among the shells and pebbles, and there was an acrid odor of smoke in the air. Down the beach the Belgians were working, loading rock into a small cart which looked like a tumbril, drawn by a bony white horse. They stooped as though in prayer, outlines against the brilliant sky, and as I watched, the bell from the chapel over at St Joseph's rang the Angelus. I found myself praying, praying with thanksgiving, praying with open eyes, while I watched the workers on the beach, the sunset, and listened to the sound of the waves and the scream of snowy gulls.

Later this evening the wind rose again and whistled around the house, and the noise of the sea is loud. I read now evenings until late in the night, and in my preoccupation the fire goes out, so that I have to get into bed to keep warm, clutching my books with ice-cold hands.

November: Mother sent me some of my high school books (now that I have a place of my own to keep them in) and the other day I came across these words, written on a faded slip of paper in my own writing. I do not remember writing them.

'Life would be utterly unbearable if we thought we were going nowhere, that we had nothing to look forward to. The greatest gift life can offer would be a faith in God and a hereafter. Why don't we have it? Perhaps like all gifts it must be struggled for. 'God, I believe' (or rather, 'I must believe or despair'). 'Help Thou my unbelief.' 'Take away my heart of stone and give me a heart of flesh.'

I wrote the above lines when I felt the urgent need for faith, but there were too many people passing through my life - too many activities - too much pleasure (not happiness).

I have been passing through some years of fret and strife, beauty and ugliness, days and even weeks of sadness and despair, but seldom has there been the quiet beauty and happiness I have now. I thought all those years that I had freedom, but now I feel that I had neither real freedom nor even a sense of what freedom meant.

And now, just as in my childhood, I am enchained, tied to one spot, unable to pick up and travel from one part of the country to another, from one job to another. I am enchained because I am going to have a baby. No matter how much I may sometimes wish to flee from my quiet existence, I cannot, nor will I be able to for several years. I have to accept my quiet and stillness, and accepting it, I rejoice in it.

For a long time, I had thought I could not bear a child. A book I read years ago in school, *Silas Marner*, expressed the sorrow of a mother bereft of her child, and it expressed, too, my sorrow at my childless state. Just a few months ago I read it again, with a longing in my heart for a baby. My home, I felt, was not a home without one. The simple joys of the kitchen and garden and beach brought sadness with them because I had not the companionship of a child. No matter how much one is loved or one loves, that love is lonely without a child. It is incomplete.

And now I know that I am going to have a baby.

SAINT FRANCIS OF ASSISI

THE CANTICLE OF THE CREATURES

O most high, almighty, good Lord God, to Thee belong praise, glory, honour, and all blessing!

Praised be my Lord God with all His creatures; and specially our brother the sun, who brings us the day, and who brings us the light; fair is he, and shining with a very great splendour: O Lord, to us he signifies Thee!

Praised be my Lord for our sister the moon, and for the stars, the which He has set clear and lovely in heaven.

Praised be my Lord for our brother the wind, and for air and cloud, calms and all weather, by the which Thou upholdest in life all creatures.

Praised be my Lord for our sister water, who is very serviceable unto us, and humble, and precious, and clean.

Praised be my Lord for our brother fire, through whom Thou givest us light in the darkness; and he is bright, and pleasant, and very mighty, and strong.

Praised be my Lord for our mother the earth, the which doth sustain and keep us, and bringeth forth divers fruits, and flowers of many colours, and grass.

Praised be my Lord for all those who pardon one another for His love's sake, and who endure weakness and tribulation; blessed are they who peaceably shall endure, for Thou, O most Highest, shalt give them a crown.

Praised be my Lord for our sister, the death of the body, from whom no man escapeth. Woe to him who dieth in mortal sin! Blessed are they who are found walking by Thy most holy will, for the second death shall have no power to do them harm.

Praise ye, and bless ye the Lord, and give thanks unto Him, and serve Him with great humility.

TRANSLATION: MATTHEW ARNOLD

LOVE BADE ME WELCOME

GEORGE HERBERT

LOVE

Love bade me welcome: yet my soul drew back,
      Guilty of dust and sin.
But quick-eyed Love, observing me grow slack
      From my first entrance in,
Drew nearer to me, sweetly questioning,
      If I lacked anything.

A guest, I answered, worthy to be here:
      Love said, You shall be he.
I the unkind, ungrateful? Ah my dear,
      I cannot look on thee.
Love took my hand, and smiling did reply,
      Who made the eyes but I?

Truth Lord, but I have marred them: let my shame
      Go where it doth deserve.
And know you not, says Love, who bore the blame?
      My dear, then I will serve.
You must sit down, says Love, and taste my meat:
      So I did sit and eat.

SIMONE WEIL

WAITING ON GOD

In 1937 I had two marvellous days at Assisi. There, alone in the little twelfth-century Romanesque chapel of Santa Maria degli Angeli, an incomparable marvel of purity where Saint Francis often used to pray, something stronger than I was compelled me for the first time in my life to go down on my knees.

In 1938 I spent ten days at Solesmes, from Palm Sunday to Easter Tuesday, following all the liturgical services. I was suffering from splitting headaches; each sound hurt me like a blow; by an extreme effort of concentration I was able to rise above this wretched flesh, to leave it to suffer by itself, heaped up in a corner, and to find a pure and perfect joy in the unimaginable beauty of the chanting and the words. This experience enabled me by analogy to get a better understanding of the possibility of loving divine love in the midst of affliction. It goes without saying that in the course of these services the thought of the Passion of Christ entered into my being once and for all.

There was a young English Catholic there from whom I gained my first idea of the supernatural power of the Sacraments because of the truly angelic radiance with which he seemed to be clothed after going to communion. Chance – or I always prefer saying chance rather than Providence – made of him a messenger to me. For he told me of the existence of those English poets of the seventeenth century who are named metaphysical. In reading them later on, I discovered the poem of which I read you what is unfortunately a very inadequate translation. It is called 'Love'. I learnt it by heart. Often, at the culminating point of a violent headache, I make myself say it over, concentrating all my attention upon it and clinging with all my soul to the tenderness it enshrines. I used to think I was merely reciting it as a beautiful poem, but without my knowing it the recitation had the virtue of a prayer. It was during one of these recitations that, as I told you, Christ himself came down and took possession of me.

In my arguments about the insolubility of the problem of God I had never foreseen the possibility of that, of a real contact, person to person, here below, between a human being and God. I had vaguely heard tell of things of this kind, but I had never believed in them. In the *Fioretti* the accounts of apparitions rather put me off if anything, like the miracles in the Gospel. Moreover, in this sudden possession of me by Christ, neither my senses nor my imagination had any part; I only felt in the midst of my suffering the presence of a love, like that which one can read in the smile on a beloved face.

I had never read any mystical works because I had never felt any call to read them. In reading as in other things I have always striven to practise obedience. There is nothing more favourable to intellectual progress, for as far as possible I only read what I am hungry for, at the moment when I have an appetite for it, and then I do not read, I *eat*. God in his mercy had prevented me from reading the mystics, so that it should be evident to me that I had not invented this absolutely unexpected contact.

Yet I still half refused, not my love but my intelligence. For it seemed to me certain, and I still think so to-day, that one can never wrestle enough with God if one does so out of pure regard for the truth. Christ likes us to prefer truth to him because, before being Christ, he is truth. If one turns aside from him to go towards the truth, one will not go far before falling into his arms.

After this I came to feel that Plato was a mystic, that all the Iliad is bathed in Christian light, and that Dionysus and Osiris are in a certain sense Christ himself; and my love was thereby re-doubled.

I never wondered whether Jesus was or was not the incarnation of God; but in fact I was incapable of thinking of him without thinking of him as God.

SOLOMON (ATTRIB.)

THE SONG OF SONGS

(VERSION FROM THE *KING JAMES BIBLE*)

CHAPTER 1

The song of songs, which is Solomon's.

Let him kiss me with the kisses of his mouth: for thy love is better than wine.

Because of the savour of thy good ointments thy name is as ointment poured forth, therefore do the virgins love thee.

Draw me, we will run after thee: the king hath brought me into his chambers: we will be glad and rejoice in thee, we will remember thy love more than wine: the upright love thee.

I am black but comely, O ye daughters of Jerusalem, as the tents of Kedar, as the curtains of Solomon.

Look not upon me, because I am black, because the sun hath looked upon me: my mother's children were angry with me; they made me the keeper of the vineyards: but mine own vineyard have I not kept.

Tell me, O thou whom my soul loveth, where thou feedest, where thou makest thy flock to rest at noon: for why should I be as one that turneth aside by the flocks of thy companions?

If thou know not, O thou fairest among women, go thy way forth by the footsteps of the flock, and feed thy kids beside the shepherds' tents.

I have compared thee, O my love, to a company of horses in Pharaoh's chariots.

Thy cheeks are comely with rows of jewels, thy neck with chains of gold.

We will make thee borders of gold with studs of silver.

While the king sitteth at his table, my spikenard sendeth forth the smell thereof.

A bundle of myrrh is my well-beloved unto me: he shall lie all night betwixt my breasts.

My beloved is unto me as a cluster of camphire in the vineyards of En-gedi.

Behold, thou art fair my love; behold, thou art fair, thou hast doves' eyes.

Behold, thou art fair, my beloved, yea, pleasant: also our bed is green.

The beams of our house are cedar, and our rafters of fire.

CHAPTER 2

I am the rose of Sharon, and the lily of the valleys.

As the lily among thorns, so is my love among the daughters.

As the apple tree among the trees of the wood, so is my beloved among the sons. I sat down under his shadow with great delight, and his fruit was sweet to my taste.

He brought me to the banqueting house, and his banner over me was love.

Stay me with flagons, comfort me with apples: for I am sick of love.

His left hand is under my head, and his right hand doth embrace me.

I charge you, O ye daughters of Jerusalem, by the roes, and by the hinds of the field, that ye stir not up, nor awake my love, till he please.

The voice of my beloved! behold, he cometh leaping upon the mountains, skipping upon the hills.

My beloved is like a roe or a young hart: behold, he standeth behind our wall, he looketh forth at the windows, shewing himself through the lattice.

My beloved spake, and said unto me. Rise up, my love, my fair one, and come away.

For, lo, the winter is past, the rain is over and gone;

The flowers appear on the earth; the time of the singing of birds is come, and the voice of the turtle is heard in our land;

The fig tree putteth forth her green figs, and the vines with the tender grape give a good smell. Arise, my love, my fair one, and come away.

O my dove, that art in the clefts of the rock, in the secret places of the stairs, let me see thy countenance, let me hear thy voice; for sweet *is* thy voice, and thy countenance is comely.

Take us the foxes, the little foxes, that spoil the vines: for our vines have tender grapes.

My beloved is mine, and I am his: he feedeth among the lilies.

Until the day break, and the shadows flee away, turn, my beloved, and be thou like a roe or a young hart upon the mountains of Bether.

CHAPTER 3

By night on my bed I sought him whom my soul loveth: I sought him, but I found him not.

I will rise now, and go about the city in the streets, and in the broad ways I will seek him whom my soul loveth: I sought him, but I found him not.

The watchmen that go about the city found me: to whom I said,

Saw ye him whom my soul loveth?

It was but a little that I passed from them, but I found him whom my soul loveth: I held him, and would not let him go, until I had brought him into my mother's house, and into the chamber of her that conceived me.

I charge you, O ye daughters of Jerusalem, by the roes, and by the hinds of the field, that ye stir not up, nor awake my love, till he please.

Who is this that cometh out of the wilderness like pillars of smoke, perfumed with myrrh and frankincense, with all powders of the merchant?

Behold his bed, which is Solomon's: threescore valiant men are about it, of the valiant of Israel.

They all hold swords, being expert in war: every man hath his sword upon his thigh because of fear in the night.

King Solomon made himself a chariot of the wood of Lebanon.

He made the pillars thereof of silver, the bottom thereof of gold, the covering of it of purple, the midst thereof being paved with love, for the daughters of Jerusalem.

Go forth, O ye daughters of Zion, and behold king Solomon with the crown wherewith his mother crowned him in the day of his espousals, and in the day of the gladness of his heart.

CHAPTER 4

Behold, thou art fair, my love; behold, thou art fair; thou hast doves' eyes within thy locks: thy hair is as a flock of goats, that appear from mount Gilead.

Thy teeth are like a flock of sheep that are even shorn, which came up from the washing; whereof every one bear twins, and none is barren among them,

Thy lips are like a thread of scarlet, and thy speech is comely: thy temples are like a piece of a pomegranate within thy locks.

Thy neck is like the tower of David builded for an armoury, whereon there hang a thousand bucklers, all shields of mighty men.

Thy two breasts are like two young roes that are twins, which feed among the lilies.

Until the day break, and the shadows flee away, I will get me to the mountain of myrrh, and to the hill of frankincense.

Thou art all fair, my love; there is no spot in thee.

Come with me from Lebanon, my spouse, with me from Lebanon:

look from the top of Amana, from the top of Shenir and Hermon, from the lions' dens, from the mountains of the leopards.

Thou hast ravished my heart, my sister, my spouse; thou hast ravished my heart with one of thine eyes, with one chain of thy neck.

How fair is thy love, my sister *my* spouse! how much better is thy love than wine! and the smell of thine ointments than all spices!

Thy lips, O my spouse, drop as the honeycomb: honey and milk are under thy tongue; and the smell of thy garments is like the smell of Lebanon.

A garden enclosed is my sister, my spouse; a spring shut up, a fountain sealed.

Thy plants are an orchard of pomegranates, with pleasant fruits; camphire with spikenard,

Spikenard and saffron; calamus and cinnamon, with all trees of frankincense; myrrh and aloes, with all the chief spices:

A fountain of gardens, a well of living waters, and streams from Lebanon.

Awake, O north wind; and come, thou south; blow upon my garden, that the spices thereof may flow out.

Let my beloved come into his garden, and eat his pleasant fruits.

CHAPTER 5

I am come into my garden, my sister, *my* spouse: I have gathered my myrrh with my spice; I have eaten my honeycomb with my honey; I have drunk my wine with my milk: eat, O friends; drink, yea, drink abundantly, O beloved.

I sleep, but my heart waketh: it is the voice of my beloved that knocketh, saying, Open to me, my sister, my love, my dove, my undefiled: for my head is filled with dew, and my locks with the drops of the nights.

I have put off my coat; how shall I put it on? I have washed my feet; how shall I defile them?

My beloved put in his hand by the hole of the door, and my bowels were moved for him.

I rose up to open to my beloved; and my hands dropped with myrrh, and my fingers with sweet smelling myrrh, upon the handles of the lock.

I opened to my beloved; but my beloved had withdrawn himself, and was gone: my soul failed when he spake: I sought him, but I could not find him; I called him, but he gave me no answer.

The watchmen that went about the city found me, they smote me, they wounded me; the keepers of the walls took away my veil from me.

I charge you, O daughters of Jerusalem, if ye find my beloved, that ye tell him that I am sick of love.

What is thy beloved more than another beloved, O thou fairest among women? what is thy beloved more than another beloved, that thou dost so charge us?

My beloved is white and ruddy, the chiefest among ten thousand.

His head is as the most fine gold, his locks are bushy, and black as a raven.

His eyes are as the eyes of doves by the rivers of waters, washed with milk, and fitly set.

His cheeks are as a bed of spices, as sweet flowers: his lips like lilies dropping sweet smelling myrrh.

His hands are as gold rings set with the beryl: his belly is as bright ivory overlaid with sapphires.

His legs are as pillars of marble, set upon sockets of fine gold: his countenance is as Lebanon, excellent as the cedars.

His mouth is most sweet: yea, he *is* altogether lovely. This *is* my beloved, and this is my friend, O daughters of Jerusalem.

CHAPTER 6

Whither is thy beloved gone, O thou fairest among women? whither is thy beloved turned aside? that we may seek him with thee.

My beloved is gone down into his garden, to the beds of spices, to feed in the gardens, and to gather lilies.

I am my beloved's, and my beloved is mine: he feedeth among the lilies.

Thou art beautiful, O my love, as Tirzah, comely as Jerusalem, terrible as an army with banners.

Turn away thine eyes from me, for they have overcome me: thy hair is as a flock of goats that appear from Gilead.

Thy teeth are as a flock of sheep which go up from the washing, whereof every one beareth twins, and there is not one barren among them.

As a piece of a pomegranate are thy temples within thy locks.

There are threescore queens, and fourscore concubines, and virgins without number.

My dove, my undefiled is but one; she is the only one of her mother, she is the choice one of her that bare her. The daughters saw her, and blessed her; yea, the queens and the concubines, and they praised her.

Who is she that looketh forth as the morning, fair as the moon, clear as the sun, and terrible as an army with banners?

I went down into the garden of nuts to see the fruits of the valley, and to see whether the vine flourished, and the pomegranates budded.

Or ever I was aware, my soul made me like the chariots of Amminadib.

Return, return, O Shulamite; return, return, that we may look upon thee. What will ye see in the Shulamite? As it were the company of two armies.

CHAPTER 7

How beautiful are thy feet with shoes,

O prince's daughter! the joints of thy thighs are like jewels, the work of the hands of a cunning workman.

Thy navel *is* like a round goblet, which wanteth not liquor: thy belly is like an heap of wheat set about with lilies.

Thy two breasts are like two young roes that are twins.

Thy neck is as a tower of ivory; thine eyes like the fishpools in Heshbon, by the gate of Bath-rabbim: thy nose is as the tower of Lebanon which looketh toward Damascus.

Thine head upon thee is like Carmel, and the hair of thine head like purple; the king is held in the galleries.

How fair and how pleasant art thou, O love, for delights!

This thy stature is like to a palm tree, and thy breasts to clusters of grapes.

I said, I will go up to the palm tree, I will take hold of the boughs thereof: now also thy breasts shall be as clusters of the vine, and the smell of thy nose like apples;

And the roof of thy mouth like the best wine for my beloved, that goeth down sweetly, causing the lips of those that are asleep to speak.

I am my beloved's, and his desire is toward me.

Come, my beloved, let us go forth into the field; let us lodge in the villages.

Let us get up early to the vineyards; let us see if the vine flourish, whether the tender grape appear, and the pomegranates bud forth: there will I give thee my loves.

The mandrakes give a smell, and at our gates are all manner of pleasant fruits, new and old, which I have laid up for thee, O my beloved.

CHAPTER 8

O That thou wert as my brother, that sucked the breasts of my mother! when I should find thee without, I would kiss thee; yea, I should not be despised.

I would lead thee, and bring thee into my mother's house, who would instruct me: I would cause thee to drink of spiced wine of the juice of my pomegranate.

His left hand should be under my head, and his right hand should embrace me.

I charge you, O daughters of Jerusalem, that ye stir not up, nor awake my love, until he please.

Who is this that cometh up from the wilderness, leaning upon her beloved? I raised thee up under the apple tree: there thy mother brought thee forth: there she brought thee forth that bare thee.

Set me as a seal upon thine heart, as a seal upon thine arm: for love is strong as death; jealousy is cruel as the grave: the coals thereof are coals of fire, which hath most vehement flame.

Many waters cannot quench love, neither can the floods drown it: if a man would give all the substance of his house for love, it would utterly be condemned.

We have a little sister, and she hath no breasts: what shall we do for our sister in the day when she shall be spoken for?

If she be a wall, we will build upon her a palace of silver: and if she be a door, we will enclose her with boards of cedar.

I am a wall, and my breasts like towers: then was I in his eyes as one that found favour.

Solomon had a vineyard at Baalhamon; he let out the vineyard unto keepers; every one for the fruit thereof was to bring a thousand pieces of silver.

My vineyard, which is mine, is before me: thou, O Solomon, must have a thousand, and those that keep the fruit thereof two hundred.

Thou that dwellest in the gardens, the companions hearken to thy voice: cause me to hear it.

Make haste, my beloved, and be thou like to a roe or to a young hart upon the mountains of spices.

THOMAS MERTON

In Louisville, at the corner of Fourth and Walnut, in the centre of the shopping district, I was suddenly overwhelmed with the realisation that I loved all those people, that they were mine and I theirs, that we could not be alien to one another even though we were total strangers. It was like waking from a dream of separateness, of spurious self-isolation in a special world, the world of renunciation and supposed holiness. The whole illusion of a separate holy existence is a dream. Not that I question the reality of my vocation, or of my monastic life: but the conception of 'separation from the world' that we have in the monastery too easily presents itself as a complete illusion: the illusion that by making vows we become a different species of being, pseudoangels, 'spiritual men,' men of interior life, what have you.

Certainly these traditional values are very real, but their reality is not of an order outside everyday existence in a contingent world, nor does it entitle one to despise the secular: though 'out of the world' we are in the same world as everybody else, the world of the bomb, the world of race hatred, the world of technology, the world of mass media, big business, revolution, and all the rest. We take a different attitude to all these things, for we belong to God. Yet so does everybody else belong to God. We just happen to be conscious of it, and to make a profession out of this consciousness. But does that entitle us to consider ourselves different, or even *better*, than others? The whole idea is preposterous.

This sense of liberation from an illusory difference was such a relief and such a joy to me that I almost laughed out loud. And I suppose my happiness could have taken form in the words: 'Thank God, thank God that I *am* like other men, that I am only a man among others.' To think that for sixteen or seventeen years I have been taking seriously this pure illusion that is implicit in so much of our monastic thinking.

It is a glorious destiny to be a member of the human race, though it is a race dedicated to many absurdities and one which makes many terrible mistakes: yet, with all that, God Himself gloried in becoming a member of the human race. A member of the human race! To think that such a common-place realisation should suddenly seem like news that one holds the winning ticket in a cosmic sweepstake.

I have the immense joy of being *man*, a member of a race in which God Himself became incarnate. As if the sorrows and stupidities of the human condition could overwhelm me, now I realise what we all are. And if only everybody could realise this! But it cannot be explained. There is no way of telling people that they are all waking around shining like the sun.

This changes nothing in the sense and value of my solitude, for it is in fact the function of solitude to make one realise such things with a clarity that would be impossible to anyone completely immersed in the other cares, the other illusions, and all the automatisms of a tightly collective existence. My solitude, however, is not my own, for I see now how much it belongs to them – and that I have a responsibility for it in their regard, not just in my own. It is because I am one with them that I owe it to them to be alone, and when I am alone they are not 'they' but my own self. There are no strangers!

Then it was as if I suddenly saw the secret beauty of their hearts, the depths of their hearts where neither sin nor desire nor self-knowledge can reach, the core of their reality, the person that each one is in God's eyes. If only they could all see themselves as they really *are*. If only we could see each other that way all the time. There would be no more war, no more hatred, no more cruelty, no more greed . . . I suppose the big problem would be that we would fall down and worship each other. But this cannot be *seen*, only believed and 'understood' by a peculiar gift.

Again, that expression, *le point vierge*, (I cannot translate it) comes in here. At the centre of our being is a point of nothingness which is untouched by sin and by illusion, a point of pure truth, a point or spark which belongs entirely to God, which is never at our disposal, from which God disposes of our lives, which is inaccessible to the fantasies of our own mind or the brutalities of our own will. This little point of nothingness and of *absolute poverty* is the pure glory of God in us. It is so to speak His name written in us, as our poverty, as our indigence, as our dependence, as our sonship. It is like a pure diamond, blazing with the invisible light of heaven. It is in everybody, and if we could see it we would see these billions of points of light coming together in the face and blaze of a sun that would make all the darkness and cruelty of life vanish. I have no programme for this seeing. It is only given. But the gate of heaven is everywhere.

JOHN DONNE

AIRE AND ANGELS

Twice or thrice had I loved thee,
Before I knew thy face or name;
So in a voice, so in a shapelesse flame,
Angells affect us oft, and worship'd bee;
    Still when, to where thou wert, I came,
Some lovely glorious nothing I did see.
    But since my soule, whose child love is,
Takes limmes of flesh, and else could nothing doe,
    More subtile than the parent is,
Love must not be, but take a body too,
    And therefore what thou wert, and who,
I bid Love aske, and now
That it assume thy body, I allow,
And fixe it selfe in thy lip, eye, and brow.

Whilst thus to ballast love, I thought,
And so more steddily to have gone,
With wares which would sinke admiration,
I saw, I had loves pinnace overfraught,
    Ev'ry thy haire for love to worke upon
Is much too much, some fitter must be sought;
    For, nor in nothing, nor in things
Extreme, and scatt'ring bright, can love inhere;
    Then as an Angell, face, and wings
Of aire, not pure as it, yet pure doth weare,
    So thy love may be my loves spheare;
    Just such disparitie
As is twixt Aire and Angells puritie,
'Twixt womens love, and mens will ever bee.

DIETRICH BONHOEFFER

EVERYTHING HAS ITS TIME

I believe that we ought so to love and trust God in our *lives*, and in
all the good things that he sends us, that when the time comes (but
not before!) we may go to him with love, trust, and joy. But, to put
it plainly, for a man in his wife's arms to be hankering after the
other world is, in mild terms, a piece of bad taste, and not God's
will. We ought to find and love God in what he actually gives us; if
it pleases him to allow us to enjoy some overwhelming earthly
happiness, we mustn't try to be more pious than God himself and
allow our happiness to be corrupted by presumption and arrogance,
and by unbridled religious fantasy which is never satisfied with what
God gives. God will see to it that the man who finds him in his
earthly happiness and thanks him for it does not lack reminder that
earthly things are transient, that it is good for him to attune his
heart to what is eternal, and that sooner or later there will be times
when he can say in all sincerity, 'I wish I were home.' But everything
has its time, and the main thing is that we keep step with God, and
do not keep pressing on a few steps ahead – nor keep dawdling a
step behind. It's presumptuous to want to have everything at once
– matrimonial bliss, the cross, and the heavenly Jerusalem, where
they neither marry nor are given in marriage. 'For everything there
is a season' (Eccles. 3.1); everything has its time: 'a time to weep,
and a time to laugh; . . . a time to embrace, and a time to refrain
from embracing; . . . a time to rend, and a time to sew; . . . and God
seeks again what is past.

JULIAN OF NORWICH

LOVE WAS HIS MEANING

For Charity pray we all; [together] with *God's* working, thanking, trusting, enjoying. For thus will our good Lord be prayed to, as by the understanding that I took of all His own meaning and of the sweet words where He saith full merrily: *I am the Ground of thy beseeching.* For truly I saw and understood in our Lord's meaning that He shewed it for that He willeth to have it known more than it is: in which knowing He will give us grace to love Him and cleave to Him. For He beholdeth His heavenly treasure with so great love on earth that He willeth to give us more light and solace in heavenly joy, in drawing to Him of our hearts, for sorrow and darkness which we are in.

And from that time that it was shewed I desired oftentimes to learn what was our Lord's meaning. And fifteen years after, and more, I was answered in ghostly understanding, saying thus: *Wouldst thou learn thy Lord's meaning in this thing? Learn it well: Love was His meaning. Who shewed it thee? Love. What shewed He thee? Love. Wherefore shewed it He? For Love. Hold thee therein and thou shalt learn and know more in the same. But thou shalt never know nor learn therein other thing without end.* Thus was I learned that Love was our Lord's meaning.

And I saw full surely that ere God made us He loved us; which love was never slacked, nor ever shall be. And in this love He hath done all his works; and in this love He hath made all things profitable to us; and in this love our life is everlasting. In our making we had beginning; but the love wherein He made us was in Him from without beginning: in which love we have our beginning. And all this shall we see in God, without end.

SOUNDS AND SIGHTS

JOHN BETJEMAN

BELLS

Let us enter the church by the tower door and climb to the ringing chamber where the ropes hang through holes in the roof. Nowhere outside England except for a very few towers in the rest of the British Isles, America and the Dominions, are bells rung so well. The carillons of the Netherlands and of Bourneville are not bell ringing as understood in England. Carillon ringing is done either by means of a cylinder worked on the barrel-organ and musical-box principle, or by keyed notes played by a musician. Carillon bells are sounded by pulling the clapper to the rim of the bell. This is called chiming, and it is not ringing.

Bell ringing in England is known among ringers as 'the exercise', rather as the rearing and training of pigeons is known among the pigeon fraternity as 'the fancy'. It is a classless folk art which has survived in the church despite all arguments about doctrine and the diminution of congregations. In many a church when the parson opens with the words 'Dearly beloved brethren, the Scripture moveth us in sundry place . . . ' one may hear the tramp of the ringers descending the newel stair into the refreshing silence of the graveyard. Though in some churches they may come in later by the main door and sit in the pew marked 'Ringers Only', in others they will not be seen again, the sweet melancholy notes of 'the exercise' floating out over the Sunday chimney-pots having been their contribution to the glory of God.

A belfry where ringers are keen has the used and admired look of a social club. There, above the little bit of looking-glass in which the ringers slick their hair and straighten their ties before stepping down into the outside world, you will find blackboards with gilded lettering proclaiming past peals rung for hours at a stretch. In another place will be the rules of the tower written in a clerkly hand . . . Many country towers have six bells. Not all these bells are medieval. Most were cast in the seventeenth, eighteenth or nineteenth centuries when change-ringing was becoming a country exercise. And the older bells will have been re-cast during that time, to bring them into tune with the new ones. They are likely to have been again re-cast in modern times, and the ancient inscription preserved and welded on to the re-cast bell. Most counties have elaborately produced monographs about their church bells. The older bells have beautiful lettering sometimes, as at Somerby, and South Somercotes in Lincolnshire, where they are inscribed with initial letters decorated with figures so that they look like illuminated initials from old manuscripts interpreted in relief on metal. The English love for Our Lady survived in inscriptions on church bells long after the Reformation, as did the use of Latin. Many eighteenth and even early nineteenth-century bells have Latin inscriptions. A rich collection of varied dates may be seen by struggling about on the wooden cage in which the bells hang among the bat-droppings in the tower.

Many local customs survive in the use of bells. In some places a curfew is rung every evening; in others a bell is rung at five in the morning during Lent. Fanciful legends have grown up about why they are rung, but their origin can generally be traced to the divine offices. The passing bell is rung differently from district to district. Sometimes the years of the deceased are tolled, sometimes the ringing is three strokes in succession followed by a pause. There are instances of the survival of prayers for the departed where the bell is tolled as soon as the news of the death of a parishioner reaches the incumbent.

Who has heard a muffled peal and remained unmoved? Leather bags are tied to one side of the clapper and the bells ring alternately loud and soft, the soft being an echo, as though in the next world, of the music we hear on earth.

I make no apology for writing so much about church bells. They ring through our literature, as they do over our meadows and roofs and few remaining elms. Some may hate them for their melancholy, but they dislike them chiefly, I think, because they are reminders of Eternity. In an age of faith they were messengers of consolation.

DIETRICH BONHOEFFER

HEARING THE BELLS

TO HIS PARENTS SUNDAY, 3 JULY 1943

When the bells of the prison chapel start ringing at about six o'clock on a Saturday evening, that is the best time to write home. It's remarkable what power church bells have over human beings, and how deeply they can affect us. So many of our life's experiences gather round them. All discontent, ingratitude, and selfishness melt away, and in a moment we are left with only our pleasant memories hovering round us like gracious spirits. I always think first of those quiet summer evenings in Friedrichsbrunn, then of all the different parishes that I have worked in, then of all our family occasions, weddings, christenings, and confirmations - tomorrow my godchild is being confirmed! - I really cannot count all the memories that come alive to me, and they all inspire peace, thankfulness, and confidence. If only one could help other people more! . . .

Just to keep you up to date with things, and not because I think that it's really worth mentioning, I ought to report my lumbago. It's not bad, but it's already lasted more than three weeks; it's a bit of a nuisance. The stone floor is probably the cause. There is everything imaginable here, ray treatment and footbaths, but nothing is any use.

I've now been in prison three months. I remember hearing Schlatter say, in his lectures on ethics, that it was one of the duties of a Christian citizen to take it patiently if he were held for investigation. That meant nothing to me at the time, but in the past few weeks I have thought of it several times, and now we must wait calmly and patiently as long as we have to, just as we have done up to now. I am dreaming more than ever that I have been released and am back home with you.

The day lilies have been simply lovely; their cups open slowly in the morning and bloom only for a day; and the next morning there are fresh ones to take their place. The day after tomorrow they will all be over . . .

WILLIAM CARLETON

LOUGH DERG

As soon as we ascended the hill, the whole scene was instantly before us: a large lake, surrounded by an amphitheatre of mountains, bleak, uncomfortable, and desolate. In the lake itself, about half a mile from the edge next us, was to be seen the 'Island,' with two or three slated houses on it, naked and unplastered, as desolate-looking almost as the mountains. A little range of exceeding low hovels, which a dwarf could scarcely enter without stooping, appeared to the left; and the eye could rest on nothing more, except a living mass of human beings crawling slowly about. The first thing the pilgrim does when he gets a sight of the lake is to prostrate himself, kiss the earth, and then on his knees offer up three *Paters* and *Aves* and a 'Creed' for the favour of being permitted to see this blessed place. When this is over, he descends to the lake, and after paying tenpence to the ferryman, is rowed over to the Purgatory.

When the whole view was presented to me, I stood for some time to contemplate it; and I cannot better illustrate the reaction which took place in my mind than by saying that it resembles that awkward inversion which a man's proper body experiences when, on going to pull something from which he expects a marvellous resistance, it comes with him at a touch, and the natural consequence is that he finds his head down and his heels up. That which dashed the whole scene from the dark elevation in which the romance of devotion had placed it was the appearance of slated houses, and of the smoke that curled from the hovels and the prior's residence. This at once brought me back to humanity; and the idea of roasting meat, boiling pots, and dressing dinners, dispossessed every fine and fearful image which had floated through my imagination for the last twelve hours. In fact, allowing for the difference of situation, it nearly resembled John's Well, or James's Fair, when beheld at a distance, turning the slated houses into inns, and the hovels into tents. A certain idea, slight, untraceable, and involuntary, went over my brain on that occasion, which, though it did not then cost me a single effort of reflection, I think was revived and developed at a future period of my life, and became, perhaps to a certain extent, the means of opening a wider range of thought to my mind, and of giving a new tone to my existence. Still, however, nothing except my idea of its external appearance disappointed me; I accordingly descended with the rest, and in a short time found myself among the living mass upon the island.

The first thing I did was to hand over my three cakes of oaten bread which I had got made in Petigo, tied up in a handkerchief, as well as my hat and second shirt, to the care of the owner of one of the huts; having first, by the way, undergone a second prostration on touching the island, and greeted it with fifteen holy kisses and another string of prayers. I then, according to the regulations; should commence the 'stations,' lacerated as my feet were after so long a journey; so that I had not a moment to rest. Think, therefore, what I must have suffered on surrounding a large chapel, in the direction of from east to west, over a pavement of stone spikes, every one of them making its way along my nerves and muscles to my unfortunate brain. I was absolutely stupid and dizzy with the pain, the praying, the jostling, the elbowing, the scrambling, and the uncomfortable penitential murmurs of the whole crowd. I knew not what I was about, but went through the forms in the same mechanical spirit which pervaded all present. I verily think that if mortification of the body, without conversation of the life or heart – if penance and not repentance *could* save the soul, no wretch who performed a pilgrimage here could with a good grace be damned. Out of hell the place is matchless, and if there be a purgatory in the other world, it may very well be said there is a fair rehearsal of it in the county of Donegal in Ireland!

When I commenced my station, I started from what is called the 'Beds,' and God help St Patrick if he lay upon them; they are sharp stones placed circularly in the earth, with the spike ends of them up, one circle within another; and the manner in which the pilgrim gets as far as the innermost resembles precisely that in which schoolboys enter the 'walls of Troy' upon their slates. I moved away from these upon the sharp stones with which the whole island is surfaced, keeping the chapel, or 'Prison,' as it is called, upon my right; then turning, I came round again, with a *circumbendibus*, to the spot from which I set out. During this circuit, as well as I can remember, I repeated fifty-five *Paters* and *Aves*, and five creeds or five decades; and be it known, that the fifty prayers were offered up to the Virgin Mary, and the odd five to God. I then commenced getting round the external beds, during which I repeated, I think, fifteen *Paters* and *Aves* more; and as the beds decreased in circumference, the prayers decreased in length, until a short circuit and three *Paters* and *Aves* finished the last and innermost of these blessed couches. I really forget how many times each day the prison and these beds are to be surrounded, and how many hundred prayers are to be repeated during the circuit, though each circuit is, in fact, making the grand tour of the island; but I never shall forget that I was the best part of a July day at it, when the soles of my feet were flayed, and the stones hot enough to broil a beef-steak. When the first day's station was over, is it necessary to say that a little rest would have been agreeable? But no, this would not suit the policy of the place: here it may be truly said that there is no rest for the wicked. The only luxury allowed me was the privilege of feasting upon one of my cakes (having not tasted food that blessed day until then) – upon one of my cakes, I say, and a copious supply of the water of the lake, which, to render the repast more agreeable, was made lukewarm. This was to keep my spirits up after the delicate day's labour I had gone through, and to cheer me against the pleasant prospect of a hard night's praying without sleep, which lay in the background. But when I saw every one at this refreshing meal with a good, thick, substantial bannock, and then looked at the immateriality of my own, I could not help reverting to the woman who made them for me with a degree of vivacity not altogether in unison with the charity of a Christian. The knavish creature defrauded me of one half of the oatmeal, although I had purchased it myself in Petigo for the occasion; being determined that as I was only to get two meals in the three days, they should be such as a person could fast upon. Never was there a man more bitterly disappointed; for they were not thicker than crown-pieces, and I searched for them in my mouth to no purpose – the only thing like substance I could feel there was the warm water. At last, night came; but here to describe the horrors of what I suffered I hold myself utterly inadequate. I was wedged in a shake-down bed with seven others, one of whom was a Scotch Papist – another a man with a shrunk leg, who wore a crutch – all afflicted with that disease which northern men that feed on oatmeal are liable to; and then the swarms that fell upon my skin, and probed, and stung, and fed on me! it was pressure and persecution almost insupportable, and yet such was my fatigue that sleep even here began to weigh down my eyelids.

EAVAN BOLAND

THE PILGRIM

When the nest falls in winter, birds have flown
To distant lights and hospitality.
The pilgrim, with his childhood home a ruin,
Shares their fate and, like them, suddenly
Becomes a tenant of the wintry day.
Looking back, out of the nest of stone
As it tumbles, he can see his childhood
Flying away like an evicted bird.

Underground although the ground is bare,
Summer is turning on her lights. Spruce
And larch and massive chestnut will appear
Above his head in leaf. Oedipus
Himself, cold and sightless, was aware
Of no more strife or drama at Colonus:
He became, when he could go no further,
Just an old man hoping for warm weather.

At journey's end in the waters of a shrine,
No greater thing will meet him than the shock
Of his own human face, beheaded in
The holy pool. Steadily he must look
At this unshriven thing among the bells
And offerings, and for his penance mark
How his aspiring days like fallen angels
Follow one another into the dark.

CATHERINE PHIL MacCARTHY

GOING TO KNOCK

Long before he took me
all the way on the train
with Paddy Clohessy talking
about the county team,
calf prices that spring,
cows giving the best milk
(we knew them all by name),
their conversation mellow

as an old whiskey,
I used to take down
the tiny glass basilica
from the white mantelpiece
in my parents' bedroom
and shake the water inside
to watch snow fall
in a blizzard over shoulders

of men and women
on a pilgrimage for sins,
and stand still in the room
when the electric light
blinked and dimmed –
the moment of apparition –
hearing an ocean sway
in the branches of a pine,

knowing it's dark
by starlings rummaging
in eaves of the barn
and the tick of a yard-light
is my mother going out
to close the hens,
asleep on one leg,
on the rungs of a shed.

WILLIAM OF ST THIERRY

From the moment when having come down the mountainside, I arrived at the Abbey of Clairvaux, I could sense the presence of God. By the simplicity and humility of the buildings the silent valley spoke of the simplicity and humility of those who lived there – the poor of Christ. Then as I went further into this valley full of people, of whom none was idle but all engaged in their various tasks, I realised that the silence here is as complete by day as it is by night, and apart from the noise of the work or the sweet sound of the praises of God, there is nothing to be heard. The effect of such silence in the midst of such activity on those who come here, is so profound that not only do they forbear from speaking idle and vain words, but they even maintain a reverent silence themselves. Even though the number of monks was great, each one was alone. A well-ordered charity brought it about that though the valley was filled with men, each one was alone and solitary. Just as a man whose spirit is disordered is never alone, even when by himself, but is ever in the midst of a turbulent crowd; so those who are united in the spirit and submit to the rule of silence, are always solitary and alone in their own hearts, even though they are surrounded by a crowd.

PHILIP LARKIN

CHURCH GOING

Once I am sure there's nothing going on
I step inside, letting the door thud shut.
Another church: matting, seats, and stone,
And little books; sprawlings of flowers, cut
For Sunday, brownish now; some brass and stuff
Up at the holy end; the small neat organ;
And a tense, musty, unignorable silence,
Brewed God knows how long. Hatless, I take off
My cycle-clips in awkward reverence,

Move forward, run my hand around the font.
From where I stand, the roof looks almost new –
Cleaned, or restored? Someone would know: I don't.
Mounting the lectern, I peruse a few
Hectoring large-scale verses, and pronounce
'Here endeth' much more loudly than I'd meant.
The echoes snigger briefly. Back at the door
I sign the book, donate an Irish sixpence,
Reflect the place was not worth stopping for.

Yet stop I did: in fact I often do,
And always end much at a loss like this,
Wondering what to look for; wondering, too,
When churches fall completely out of use
What we shall turn them into, if we shall keep
A few cathedrals chronically on show,
Their parchment, plate and pyx in locked cases,
And let the rest rent-free to rain and sheep.
Shall we avoid them as unlucky places?

Or, after dark, will dubious women come
To make their children touch a particular stone;
Pick simples for a cancer; or on some
Advised night see walking a dead one?
Power of some sort or other will go on
In games, in riddles, seemingly at random;

But superstition, like belief, must die,
And what remains when disbelief has gone?
Grass, weedy pavement, brambles, buttress, sky,

A shape less recognisable each week,
A purpose more obscure. I wonder who
Will be the last, the very last, to seek
This place for what it was; one of the crew
That tap and jot and know what rood-lofts were?
Some ruin-bibber, randy for antique,
Or Christmas-addict, counting on a whiff
Of gown-and-bands and organ-pipes and myrrh?
Or will he be my representative,

Bored, uninformed, knowing the ghostly silt
Dispersed, yet tending to this cross of ground
Through suburb scrub because it held unspilt
So long and equably what since is found
Only in separation – marriage, and birth,
And death, and thoughts of these – for which was built
This special shell? For, though I've no idea
What this accoutred frowsty barn is worth,
It pleases me to stand in silence here;

A serious house on serious earth it is,
In whose blent air all our compulsions meet,
Are recognised, and robed as destinies.
And that much never can be obsolete,
Since someone will forever be surprising
A hunger in himself to be more serious,
And gravitating with it to this ground,
Which, he once heard, was proper to grow wise in,
If only that so many dead lie round.

KINDLING THE FIRE

ANONYMOUS

I SING OF A MAIDEN

I sing of a Maiden
 That is makeless;
King of all kings
 To her Son she ches.
He came also still
 There His Mother was,
As dew in April
 That falleth on the grass.
He came also still
 To his Mother's bower,
As dew in April
 That falleth on the flower.
He came also still
 There His Mother lay,
As dew in April
 That falleth on the spray.
Mother and maiden
 Was never none but she;
Well may such a Lady
 God's Mother be.

PADRAIC FALLON

MATER DEI

In March the seed
Fell, when the month leaned over, looking
Down into her valley.
And none but the woman knew it where she sat
In the tree of her veins and tended him
The red and ripening Adam of the year.

Her autumn was late and human.
Trees were nude, the lights were on the pole
All night when he came,
Her own man;
In the cry of a child she sat, not knowing
That this was a stranger.

Milk ran wild
Across the heavens. Imperiously He
Sipped at the delicate beakers she proffered him.
How was she to know
How huge a body she was, how she corrected
The very tilt of the earth on its new course.

GEORGE MACKAY BROWN

OUR LADY OF THE WAVES

The twenty brothers of Eynhallow
Have made a figure of Our Lady.
From red stone they carved her
And set her on a headland.
There spindrift salts her feet.
At dawn the brothers sang this

Blessed Lady, since midnight
We have done three things.
We have bent hooks.
We have patched a sail.
We have sharpened knives.
Yet the little silver brothers are afraid.
Bid them come to our net.
Show them our fire, our fine round plates.
Per Christum Dominum nostrum
Look mildly on our hungers.

The codling hang in a row by the wall.
At noon the brothers sang this
    Holy Mother, Una the cow
    Gives thin blue milk.
    Where is the golden thread of butter?
    The stone in the middle of the glebe
    Has deep black roots.
    We have broken three ploughs on it.
    Per Christum Dominum nostrum
    Save Una from the axe,
    Our dappled cow with large eyes.

The girls go by with pails to the byre.
At sunset the brothers sang this
    Sweet Virgin, the women of Garth
    Bring endless gifts to Brother Paul.
    They put an egg in his palm,
    They lay peats in his cowl.
    One neck is long as spilling milk.
    Brother Paul is a good lad.
    Well he brings wine and word to the priest.
    At midnight he sits by a white candle.

Paul has gnarled knees at the stone.
At midnight the brothers sang this
    Queen of Heaven, this good day
    There is a new cradle at Quoys.
    It rocks on the blue floor.
    And there is a new coffin at Hamnavoe.
    Arnor the poet lies there,

Tired of words and wounds.
In between, what is man?
A head bent over fish and bread and ale.
Outside, the long furrow.
Through a door, a board with a shape on it.

Guard the ploughs and the nets.

Star of the Sea, shine for us.

(*from* 'The Five Voyages of Arnor')

FRANCIS STUART

OUR LADY OF BIKINI

She will not come anymore,
Appearing between the lines
Of the drab story
That is all that is left us to tell,
Reciting a Magnificat,
Not even to children as at Fatima,
Lourdes or La Salette,
Not in gardens 'where apple trees lean low;
Nor her shadow fall on our poems.
Indifference is in everything we do
And the poison in Nature's veins and in our hearts
As the forests are starting to wither,
Not with autumn's ancient enchantment
But under the disc of the black sun
Set in the heavens for a sign
And a foretaste of how it will be
When the powerful inherit a dead planet.

ANONYMOUS

KINDLING THE FIRE

I will raise the hearth-fire
As Mary would.
The encirclement of Bride and of Mary
On the fire, and on the floor,
And on the household all.

Who are they on the bare floor?
John and Peter and Paul.
Who are they by my bed?
The lovely Bride and her Fosterling.
Who are those watching over my sleep?
The fair loving Mary and her Lamb.
Who is that anear me?
The King of the sun, He himself it is.
Who is that at the back of my head?
The Son of Life without beginning, without time.

from THE CARMINA GODELICA

SOMETHING UNDERSTOOD

LIGHT

JAMES ROOSE-EVANS

The miner with a lamp fixed to his head, enabling him to descend into the bowels of the earth and work his way along narrowing tunnels, chipping away the coal surface, is an apt image of the soul at prayer, recalling those portraits of St Dominic with a star just above his forehad, and reminding us of the Third Eye of spiritual perception. The motto of the order of St Dominic is *Dominus, illimunatio mea* – the Lord is my Light. The Dominican Order has always placed great emphasis upon the light of reason and St Thomas Aquinas, the great theologian, was one of its most shining lights.

The Lord is my light and salvation. The light of reason can only take us so far, chipping away at the darkness. There is need, too, for the light within. The miner's lamp recalls also the wise virgins who kept their lamps trimmed, who were always in a state of waiting upon the coming of the Divine Bridegroom; and our experience will teach us that, in meditation, it is indeed as though at the very centre of our being a lamp were burning. All our attention and all our concentration are needed if that small flame is not to go out. It must burn calmly, steadily, a small flame in the surrounding darkness. It is a divine spark.

As the mind becomes stilled, so we begin to enter with deep concentration the inner sanctum of our being and of the Eternal Being. There the flame flickers like a tabernacle lamp. The ceaseless distraction of thoughts is like a draught threatening to extinguish it but, as they recede there, at the edge of darkness, the light grows more steady; so that, even on those days when we feel nothing, when nothing seems to be happening, we know that far within, in the sanctuary, in the inner darkness, a vigil is being kept, and a lamp is burning. *Dominus, illimunatio mea.*

GEORGE HERBERT

PRAYER

Prayer the Church's banquet, Angels' age,
   God's breath in man returning to his birth,
   The soul in paraphrase, heart in pilgrimage,
The Christian plummet sounding heav'n and earth;
Engine against th' Almighty, sinners' tower,
   Reversed thunder, Christ-side-piercing spear,
   The six-days world-transposing in an hour,
A kind of tune, which all things hear and fear;
Softness, and peace, and joy, and love, and bliss,
   Exalted Manna, gladness of the best,
   Heaven in ordinary, man well dressed,
The milky way, the bird of Paradise,
   Church bells beyond the stars heard, the soul's blood,
   The land of spices; something understood.

SAINT TERESA OF AVILA

MIRROR AND SOUL

On one occasion, when I was reciting the Hours with the community, my soul suddenly became recollected and seemed to me to become bright all over like a mirror: no part of it – back, sides, top or bottom – but was completely bright, and in the centre of it was a picture of Christ our Lord as I generally see him. I seemed to see him in every part of my soul as clearly as in a mirror, and this mirror – I cannot explain how – was wholly sculptured in the same Lord by a most loving communication which I shall never be able to describe. This I know was a vision which, whenever I recall it, and especially after Communion, is always of great profit to me. It was explained to me that, when a soul is in mortal sin, this mirror is covered with a thick mist and remains darkened so that the Lord cannot be pictured or seen in it, though he is always present with us and gives us our being; with heretics it is as if the mirror were broken, which is much worse than being dimmed. Seeing this is very different from describing it, for it cannot be properly explained. But it has helped me a great deal and has also caused me deep regrets at the many occasions when, through my faults, my soul has become darkened and so I have been unable to see the Lord.

This vision seems to me a very beneficial one for recollected persons, for it teaches them to think of the Lord as being in the very innermost part of their soul. This is a meditation which has a lasting effect, and, as I have said on other occasions, is much more fruitful than thinking of him as outside us, as certain books do which treat of prayer, telling us where we are to seek God.

ANONYMOUS

THE CLOUD OF UNKNOWING

Just as the meditations of those who seek to live the contemplative life come without warning, so, too, do their prayers. I am thinking of their private prayers, of course, not those laid down by Holy Church. For true contemplatives could not value such prayers more, and so they use them, in the form and according to the rules laid down by the Holy Fathers before us. But their own personal prayers rise spontaneously to God, without bidding or premeditation, beforehand or during their prayer.

If they are in words, as they seldom are, then they are very few words; the fewer the better. If it is a little word of one syllable, I think it is better than if it is of two, and more in accordance with the work of the Spirit. For a contemplative should always live at the highest, topmost peak spiritually.

We can illustrate this by looking at nature. A man or woman, suddenly frightened by fire, or death, or what you will, is suddenly in his extremity of spirit driven hastily and by necessity to cry or pray for help. And how does he do it? Not, surely, with a spate of words; not even in a single word of two syllables! Why? He thinks it wastes too much time to declare his urgent need and his agitation. So he bursts out in his terror with one little word, and that of a single syllable: 'Fire!' it may be, or 'Help!'

Just as this little word stirs and pierces the ears of the hearers more quickly, so too does a little word of one syllable, when it is not merely spoken or thought, but expresses also the intention in the depth of our spirit. Which is the same as the 'height' of our spirit, for in these matters height, depth, length, and breadth all mean the same. And it pierces the ears of Almighty God more quickly than any long psalm churned out unthinkingly. That is why it is written 'Short prayer penetrates heaven.'

Why does it penetrate heaven, this short little prayer of one syllable? Surely because it is prayed with a full heart, in the height and depth and length and breadth of the spirit of him that prays it. In the height, for it is with all the might of his spirit; in the depth, for in this little syllable is contained all that the spirit knows; in the length, for should it always feel as it does now, it would always cry to God as it now cries; in the breadth, for it would extend to all men what it wills for itself.

At this time the soul understands what St Paul and all saints speak of – not fully, perhaps, but as much as one can at this stage of contemplation – and that is, what is the length and breadth and height and depth of the everlasting, all-loving, all-mighty, all-knowing God. God's everlastingness is his length; his love is his breadth; his might is his height; and his wisdom is his depth. No wonder that a soul moulded by grace into the close image and likeness of God his maker is so soon heard by God! Yes, even if it is a very sinful soul, who is as it were an enemy of God. If he through grace were to cry such a short syllable in the height, depth, length, and breadth of his spirit, he would always be heard because of this anguished cry, and be helped by God.

An example will show this. If you were to hear your deadly enemy in terror cry out from the depth of his being this little word 'Fire!' or 'Help!', you without reckoning he was your enemy, out of sheer pity aroused by his despairing cry, would rise up, even on a mid-winter night, and help him put out his fire, or quieten and ease his distress. Oh Lord! since grace can make a man so merciful as to show great mercy and pity to his enemy despite his enmity, what pity and mercy shall God have for the spiritual cry of a soul that comes from its height and depth and length and breadth! God has in his nature all that man acquires by grace. And much more, incomparably more mercy will God have, since the natural endowment of a thing makes it basically more kin to eternal things than that which is given it later by grace.

We must therefore pray in the height, depth, length, and breadth of our spirits. Not in many words, but in a little word of one syllable. What shall this word be? Surely such a word as is suited to the nature of prayer itself. And what word is that? First let us see what prayer is in itself, and then we shall know more clearly what word will best suit its nature.

In itself prayer is nothing else than a devout setting of our will in the direction of God in order to get good, and remove evil. Since all evil is summed up in sin, considered casually or essentially, when we pray with intention for the removing of evil, we should neither say, think, nor mean any more than this little word 'sin'. And if we pray with intention for the acquiring of goodness, let us pray, in word or thought or desire, no other word than 'God'. For in God is all good, for he is its beginning and its being. Do not be surprised then that I set these words before all others. If I could find any shorter words which would sum up fully the thought of good or evil as these words do, or if I had been led by God to take some other words, then I would have used those and left these. And that is my advice for you too.

But don't study these words, for you will never achieve your object so, or come to contemplation; it is never attained by study, but only by grace. Take no other words for your prayer, despite all I have said, than those that God leads you to use. Yet if God does lead you to these, my advice is not to let them go, that is, if you are using words at all in your prayer: not otherwise. They are very short words. But though shortness of prayer is greatly to be recommended here, it does not mean that the frequency of prayer is to be lessened. For as I have said, it is prayed in the length of one's spirit, so that it never stops until such time as it has full attained what it longs for. We can turn to our terrified man or woman for an example. They never stop crying their little words 'Help!' or 'Fire!' till such time as they have got all the help they need in their trouble.

PATRICK KAVANAGH

HAVING CONFESSED

Having confessed he feels
That he should go down on his knees and pray
For forgiveness for his pride, for having
Dared to view his soul from the outside.
Lie at the heart of the emotion, time
Has its own work to do. We must not anticipate
Or awaken for a moment. God cannot catch us
Unless we stay in the unconscious room
Of our hearts. We must be nothing,
Nothing that God may make us something.
We must not touch the immortal material
We must not daydream to-morrow's judgement –
God must be allowed to surprise us.
We have sinned, sinned like Lucifer
By this anticipation. Let us lie down again
Deep in anonymous humility and God
May find us worthy material for His hand.

THOMAS MERTON

DISTRACTIONS

If you have never had any distractions you don't know how to pray.
For the secret of prayer is a hunger for God and for the vision of
God, a hunger that lies far deeper than the level of language or
affection. And a man whose memory and imagination are
persecuting him with a crowd of useless or even evil thoughts and
images may sometimes be forced to pray far better, in the depths
of his murdered heart, than one whose mind is swimming with clear
concepts and brilliant purposes and easy acts of love.

That is why it is useless to get upset when you cannot shake
off distractions. In the first place, you must realise that they are

often unavoidable in the life of prayer. The necessity of kneeling and suffering submersion under a tidal wave of wild and inane images is one of the standard trials of the contemplative life. If you think you are obliged to stave these things off by using a book and clutching at its sentences the way a drowning man clutches at straws, you have the privilege of doing so, but if you allow your prayer to degenerate into a period of simple spiritual reading you are losing a great deal of fruit. You would profit much more by patiently resisting distractions and learning something of your own helplessness and incapacity. And if your book merely becomes an anaesthetic, far from helping your meditation, it has probably ruined it.

One reason why you have distractions is this. The mind and memory and imagination only work, in meditation, in order to bring your will into the presence of its object, which is God. Now when you have practised meditation for a few years, it is the most spontaneous thing in the world for the will to settle down to its occupation of obscurely and mutely loving God as soon as you compose yourself for prayer. Consequently the mind and memory and imagination have no real job to do. The will is busy and they are unemployed. So, after a while, the doors of your subconscious mind fall ajar and all sorts of curious figures begin to come waltzing about on the scene. If you are wise you will not pay any attention to these things: remain in simple attention to God and you keep your will peacefully directed to Him in simple desire, while the intermittent shadows of this annoying movie go about in the remote background. If you are aware of them at all it is only to realise that you refuse them.

The kind of distractions that holy people most fear are generally the most harmless of all. But sometimes pious men and women torture themselves at meditation because they imagine they are 'consenting' to the phantasms of a lewd and somewhat idiotic burlesque that is being fabricated in their imagination without their being able to do a thing to stop it. The chief reason why they suffer is that their hopeless efforts to put a stop to this parade of images generate a nervous tension which only makes everything a hundred times worse.

If they ever had a sense of humour, they have now become so nervous that it has abandoned them altogether. Yet humour is one of the things that would probably be most helpful at such a time.

There is no real danger in these things. The distractions that do harm are the ones that draw our will away from its profound and peaceful occupation with God and involve it in elaborations of projects that have been concerning us during our day's work. We are confronted by issues that really attract and occupy our wills and there is considerable danger that our meditation will break into a session of mental letter-writing or sermons or speeches or books or, worse still, plans to raise money or to take care of our health.

It will be hard for anyone who has a heavy job on his shoulders to get rid of these things. They will always remind him of what he is, and they should warn him not to get too involved in active work, because it is no use trying to clear your mind of all material things at the moment of meditation, if you do nothing to cut down the pressure of work outside that time.

But in all these things, it is the will to pray that is the essence of prayer, and the desire to find God and to see Him and to love Him is the one thing that matters. If you have desired to know Him and love Him you have already done what was expected of you and it is much better to desire God without being able to think clearly of Him, than to have marvellous thoughts about Him without desiring to enter into union with His will.

RICHARD ROLLE

SINGING INWARDLY

From the time my conversion of life and mind began until the day the door of Heaven swung back and his Face was revealed, so that my inner eye could contemplate the things that are above, and see by what way it might find the Beloved and cling to him, three years passed, all but three or four months. But the door remained open for nearly a year longer before I could really feel in my heart the warmth of eternal love.

I was sitting in a certain chapel, delighting in the sweetness of prayer or meditation, when suddenly I felt within myself an unusually pleasant heat. At first I wondered where it came from, but it was not long before I realised that it was from none of his creatures but from the Creator himself. It was, I found, more fervent and pleasant than I had ever known. But it was just over nine months before a conscious and incredibly sweet warmth kindled me, and I knew the infusion and understanding of heavenly, spiritual sounds,

sounds which pertain to the song of eternal praise, and to the sweetness of unheard melody; sounds which cannot be known or heard save by him who has received it, and who himself must be clean and separate from the things of earth.

While I was sitting in that same chapel, and repeating as best I could the night-psalms before I went in to supper, I heard, above my head it seemed, the joyful ring of psalmody, or perhaps I should say, the singing. In my prayer I was reaching out to heaven with heartfelt longing when I became aware, in a way I cannot explain, of a symphony of song, and in myself I sensed a corresponding harmony at once wholly delectable and heavenly, which persisted in my mind. Then and there my thinking itself turned into melodious song, and my meditation became a poem, and my very prayers and psalms took up the same sound. The effect of this inner sweetness was that I began to sing what previously I had spoken; only I sang inwardly, and that for my Creator. But it was not suspected by those who saw me, for if they had known they would have honoured me beyond all measure, and I should have lost part of this most lovely flower, and have fallen into desolation. Meantime wonder seized me that I should be caught up into such joy while I was still an exile, and that God should give me gifts, the like of which I did not know I could ask for, and such that I thought that not even the most holy could have received in this life. From which I deduce that they are not given for merit, but freely to whomsoever Christ wills. All the same I fancy that no one will receive them unless he has a special love for the Name of Jesus, and so honours it that he never lets it out of his mind, except in sleep. Anyone to whom this is given will, I think, achieve this very thing.

RICHARD BAXTER

PLACES OF MEDITATION

Concerning the fittest place for heavenly meditation it is sufficient to say that the most convenient is some private retirement. Our spirits need every help, and to be freed from every hindrance in the work. If in private prayer, Christ directs us to 'enter into our closet and shut the door', that 'our Father may see us in secret'; so should we do in this meditation. How often did Christ Himself retire to some mountain, or wilderness, or other solitary place! I give not this advice for occasional meditation, but for that which is set and solemn. Therefore withdraw thyself from all society, even the society of godly men, that thou mayest awhile enjoy the society of the Lord. If a student cannot study in a crowd, who exerciseth only his invention and memory, much less shouldst thou be in a crowd, who art to exercise all the powers of thy soul, and upon an object so far above nature . . .

But observe for thyself what place best agrees with thy spirit; whether within doors, or without. Isaac's example in 'going out to meditate in the field' will, I believe, best suit with most. Our Lord so much used a solitary garden that even Judas, when he came to betray Him, knew where to find Him: and though He took His disciples thither with Him, yet He was 'withdrawn from them' for more secret devotions . . . So that Christ had His accustomed place, and consequently accustomed duty, and so must we; He hath a place that is solitary, whither He retireth Himself, even from His own disciples, and so must we; His meditations go farther than His words, they affect and pierce His heart and soul, and so must ours. Only there is a wide difference in the object: Christ meditates on the sufferings that our sins had deserved, so that the wrath of His Father passed through all His soul; but we are to meditate on the glory He hath purchased, that the love of the Father, and the joy of the Spirit, may enter at our thoughts, revive our affections, and overflow our souls.

R. S. THOMAS

KNEELING

Moments of great calm,
Kneeling before an altar
Of wood in a stone church
In summer, waiting for the God
To speak; the air a staircase
For silence; the sun's light

Ringing me, as though I acted
A great rôle. And the audiences
Still; all that close throng
Of spirits waiting, as I,
For the message.
                    Prompt me, God;
But not yet. When I speak,
Though it be you who speak
Through me, something is lost.
The meaning is in the waiting.

ANONYMOUS

SEA PRAYER

Helmsman
Blest be the boat.

Crew
God the Father bless her.
Helmsman
Blest be the boat.

Crew
God the Son bless her.

Helmsman
Blest be the boat.

Crew
God the Spirit bless her.

All
God the Father,
God the Son,
God the Spirit,
Bless the boat.

Helmsman
What can befall you
And God the Father with you?

Crew
No harm can befall us.

Helmsman
What can befall you
And God the Son with you?

Crew
No harm can befall us.

Helmsman
What can befall you
And God the Spirit with you?

Crew
No harm can befall us.

All
God the Father,
God the Son,
God the Spirit,
With us eternally.

Helmsman
What can cause you anxiety
And the God of the elements over you?

Crew
No anxiety can be ours.

Helmsman
What can cause you anxiety
And the King of the elements over you?

Crew
No anxiety can be ours.

Helmsman
What can cause you anxiety
And the Spirit of the elements over you?

Crew
No anxiety can be ours.

All
The God of the elements,
The King of the elements,
The Spirit of the elements,
Close over us,
Ever eternally.

from THE *CARMINA GODELICA*

SAINT TERESA OF AVILA

WATER AND THE STAGES OF PRAYER

A beginner must look on himself as one setting out to make a garden for his Lord's pleasure, on most unfruitful soil which abounds in weeds. His Majesty roots up the weeds and will put in good plants instead. Let us reckon that this is already done when a soul decides to practise prayer and has begun to do so. We have then, as good gardeners, with God's help to make these plants grow, and to water them carefully so that they do not die, but produce flowers, which give out a good smell, to delight this Lord of ours. Then He will often come to take His pleasure in this garden and enjoy these virtues.

Now let us see how this garden is to be watered, so that we may understand what we have to do, and what labour it will cost us, also whether the gain will outweigh the effort, or how long it will take. It seems to me that the garden may be watered in four different ways. Either the water must be drawn from a well, which is very laborious; or by a water-wheel and buckets, worked by a windlass – I have sometimes drawn it in this way, which is less laborious than the other, and brings up more water – or from a stream or spring, which waters the ground much better, for the soil then retains more moisture and needs watering less often, which entails far less work for the gardener; or by heavy rain, when the Lord waters it Himself without any labour of ours; and this is an incomparably better method than all the rest.

Now to apply these four methods of watering, by which this garden is to be maintained and without which it will fail. This is my purpose, and will, I think, enable me to explain something about the four stages of prayer, to which the Lord has, in His kindness, sometimes raised my soul . . .

We may say that beginners in prayer are those who draw the water up out of the well; which is a great labour, as I have said. For they find it very tiring to keep the senses recollected, when they are used to a life of distraction. Beginners have to accustom themselves to pay no attention to what they see or hear, and to put this exercise into practice during their hours of prayer, when they must remain in solitude, thinking whilst they are alone of their past life. Although all must do this many times, the advanced as well as the beginners, all need not do so equally, as I shall explain later. At first they are distressed because they are not sure that they regret their sins. Yet clearly they do, since they have now sincerely resolved to serve God. They should endeavour to meditate on the life of Christ, and thus the intellect will grow tired. Up to this point we can advance ourselves, though with God's help of course, for without it, as everyone knows, we cannot think one good thought.

This is what I mean by beginning to draw water from the well – and God grant there may be water in it! But at least this does not depend on us, who have only to draw it up and do what we can to water the flowers. But God is so good that when for reasons known to His Majesty – and perhaps for our greater profit – He wishes the well to be dry, we, like good gardeners, must do what we can ourselves. Meanwhile He preserves the flowers without water, and in this way He makes our virtues grow. Here by water I mean tears, or if there be none, a tenderness and inward feeling of devotion. But what shall a man do here who finds that for many days on end he feels nothing but dryness, dislike, distaste and so little desire to go and draw water that he would give it up altogether if he did not remember that he is pleasing and serving the Lord of the garden; if he did not want all his service to be in vain, and if he did not also hope to gain something for all the labour of lowering the bucket so often into the well and bringing it up empty? It will often happen that he cannot so much as raise his arms to the task, or think a single good thought. For by this drawing of water I mean, of course, working with the understanding . . .

Having spoken of the effort and physical labour entailed in watering the garden, and what efforts it costs to raise the water from the well, let us now turn to the second method of drawing it which the Owner of the plot has ordained. By means of a device with a windlass, the gardener draws more water with less labour, and so is able to take some rest instead of being continuously at work. I apply this description to the prayer of quiet, which I am now going to describe.

Now the soul begins to be recollected, and here it comes into touch with the supernatural, to which it could not possibly attain by its own efforts. True, sometimes it seems to have grown weary through turning the wheel, and toiling with its mind, and filling the buckets. But in this state the level of the water is higher, and so much less labour is required than for drawing it from a well. I mean that the water is closer because grace reveals itself more clearly to the soul. This entails a gathering of the faculties within oneself so as to derive a greater savour from that pleasure. But they are not lost or asleep. The will alone is occupied in such a way that it is unconsciously taken captive. It simply consents to be God's prisoner, since it well knows how to surrender to One whom it loves. O Jesus, my Lord, how precious Your love is to us then! It binds our own love so closely to it as to leave us no liberty to love anything but you!

The other two faculties – the memory and the imagination – help the will to make itself more and more capable of enjoying this great blessing, though, on the other hand, it sometimes happens that they are a great hindrance to it, even when the will is in union. But then it should never pay attention to them but stay in its joy and quiet. For if it tried to make them recollected, both it and they might lose the way. Then they behave like doves who are not satisfied with the food given to them by the owner of the dovecote, without their working for it, and go out to seek nourishment in other places, but find so little that they come back. So these two faculties come and go, hoping that the will can give them some part of what it is enjoying. If it be the Lord's pleasure, it throws them some food and they stop; if not, they resume their search. One must reflect that these activities benefit the will; without them, the memory and the imagination might do it serious harm by trying to give it a picture of what it is enjoying. The will must be careful in its dealings with them, as I shall explain.

Everything that happens now brings very great consolation, and costs so little labour that, even if prayer is continued for some time, it brings no weariness. The intellect now works very gently and draws up a great deal more water than it drew from the well. The tears that God sends now are shed with joy; although we are conscious of them, they are not of our getting.

This water of great blessings and favours which the Lord now gives us makes the virtues grow incomparably more than they did in the previous state of prayer. Our soul is already rising from its wretched state, and receives some little intimation of the joys of heaven. It is this, I believe, that increases the growth of the virtues, and brings them closer to God – that true Virtue, from which all virtues spring. For His Majesty begins to communicate Himself to the soul, and would have it feel how He is communication Himself.

On arriving at this state, the soul begins to lose the desire for earthly things –and no wonder!

Let us now go on to speak of the third water that feeds this garden, which is flowing water from a stream or spring. This irrigates it with far less trouble, though some effort is required to direct it into the right channel. But now the Lord is pleased to help the gardener in such a way as to be, as it were, the gardener Himself. For it is He who does everything. The faculties of the soul are asleep, not entirely lost nor yet entirely conscious of how they are working. The pleasure, sweetness, and delight are incomparably more than in the previous state, for the water of grace has risen to the soul's neck, and it is powerless, knowing neither how to advance nor to retreat; what it wants is to enjoy its very great glory. It is like a man with the funeral candle in his hand, on the point of dying the death he desires. It takes unutterable delight in the enjoyment of its agony, which seems to me like nothing else but an almost complete death to all the things of this world, and a fulfilment in God. I know of no other words with which to describe or explain it. The soul does not know what to do; it cannot tell whether to speak or be silent, whether to laugh or weep. It is a glorious bewilderment, a heavenly madness, in which true wisdom is acquired, and to the soul a fulfilment most full of delight.

It is, I believe, five or six years since the Lord first granted me frequent and abundant experience of this sort of prayer; and I have never understood it or been able to explain it. I decided therefore that when I came to this place in my narrative I would say little or nothing about it. I knew very well that it was not a complete union of all the faculties, and yet it was clearly higher than the previous state of prayer. But I confess that I could not decide or understand where the difference lay.

It was your Reverence's humility, I believe, in consenting to accept help from a person as simple as I, that caused the Lord to grant me this prayer to-day, after Communion. His Majesty did not allow me to pass beyond it, but suggested these comparisons to me, teaching me how to explain this state, and what the soul must do when in it. I was indeed amazed, and understood it all in a flash. Very often I was, so to speak, bewildered and intoxicated with love, and yet could never understand how it was. I knew very well that this was God's work but I could never understand the way in which He worked here. In effect the faculties are in almost complete union, yet not so absorbed that they do not act. I am greatly delighted that I have understood it at last. Blessed be the Lord, who has given me this gift!

The faculties retain only the power of occupying themselves wholly with God. None of them seems to dare even to stir, nor can we make any one of them move without great and deliberate efforts to fix the attention on some external thing, though I do not think that at such times we can entirely succeed in doing this. Many words are then spoken in praise of the Lord. But they are disorderly, unless the Lord Himself imposes order on them. The intellect, at any rate, is of no value here. The soul longs to pour out words of praise. But it is in a sweet unrest, and cannot contain itself. Already the flowers are opening, and beginning to give of scent.

In this state the soul would have everyone behold it and – to the glory of God – know of its bliss, and help it to praise Him. It would have them partake of its joy, which is greater than it can bear alone. This reminds me of the woman in the Gospel who wanted to call, or did call her neighbours together. Such must, I think, have been the feelings of that wondrous David, the royal prophet, when he played on the harp and sang the praises of God . . .

May the Lord teach me words with which to convey some idea of the fourth water. I shall indeed need His help more now than ever before. In this state, the soul still feels that it is not altogether dead, as we may say, though it is entirely dead to the world. But, as I have said, it retains the sense to know that it is still here and to feel its solitude; and it makes use of outward manifestations to show its feelings, at least by signs. Throughout, in every stage of the prayer that I have described, the gardener performs some labour, though in these later stages the labour is accompanied by so much bliss and comfort to the soul that the soul would never willingly abandon it. So the labour is not felt as such, but as bliss.

Here there is no sense of anything but enjoyment, without any knowledge of what is being enjoyed. The soul realises that it is enjoying some good thing that contains all good things together, but it cannot comprehend this good thing. All the senses are taken up with this joy so that none of them is free to act in any way, either outwardly or inwardly. Previously, as I have said, the senses were permitted to give some indication of the great joy they feel. But now the soul enjoys incomparably more, and yet has still less power to show it. For there is no power left in the body – and the soul possesses none – by which this joy can be communicated. At such a time anything of the sort would be a great embarrassment, a torment and a disturbance of its repose. If there is really a union of all the faculties, I say, then the soul cannot make it known, even if it wants to – while actually in union I mean. If it can, then it is not in union.

How what is called union takes place and what it is, I cannot tell. It is explained in *mystical theology*, but I cannot use the proper terms; I cannot understand what *mind* is, or how it differs from *soul* or *spirit*. They all seem one to me, though the soul sometimes leaps out of itself like a burning fire that has become one whole flame and increases with great force. The flame leaps very high above the fire. Nevertheless it is not a different thing, but the same flame which is in the fire. You, sirs, with your learning will understand this. I cannot be more explicit.

I am now speaking of that rain that comes down abundantly from heaven to soak and saturate the whole garden. If the Lord never ceased to send it whenever it was needed, the gardener would certainly have leisure; and if there were no winter but always a temperate climate, there would never be a shortage of fruit and flowers, and the gardener would clearly be delighted. But this is impossible while we live, for we must always be looking out for one water when another fails. The heavenly rain very often comes down when the gardener least expects it. Yet it is true that at the beginning it almost always comes after long mental prayer. Then, as one stage succeeds another, the Lord takes up this small bird and puts it into the nest where it may be quiet. He has watched it fluttering for a long time, trying with its understanding and its will and all its strength to find God and please Him; and now He is pleased to give it its reward in this life. And what a reward! One moment of it is enough to repay all the trials it can ever have endured.

MOTHER MARIBEL OF WANTAGE

DOG-TIREDNESS

Dog-tiredness is such a lovely prayer, really, if only we would recognise it as such. Sometimes I hear, 'I'm so dog-tired when I get to chapel, I can't pray'. But what does it matter? We don't matter. Our Lord can pray just as well through a dog-tired body and mind as through a well-rested one, better perhaps. It is the same with pain and suffering of all kinds. Our advance guard on the Infirmary Wing would tell us that.

DOUBT AND CONVERSION

THE VENERABLE BEDE

THE CONVERSION OF KING EDWIN

Holding a council with the wise men, he asked of every one in particular what he thought of the new doctrine and the new worship that was presented. To which the chief of his own priests, Coifi, immediately answered:

'O king, consider what this is which is now preached to us; for I verily declare to you that the religion which we have hitherto professed has, as far as I can learn, no virtue in it. For none of your people has applied himself more diligently to the worship of our gods than I; and yet there are many who receive greater favours from you, and are more preferred than I, and are more prosperous in all their undertakings. Now if the gods were good for anything, they would rather forward me who have been more careful to serve them. It remains, therefore, that if upon examination you find those new doctrines, which are now preached among us, better and more efficacious, we receive them without any delay.'

Another of the king's chief men, approving of his words and exhortations, immediately added: 'The present life of man, O king, seems to me, in comparison with that time which is unknown to us, like to the swift flight of a sparrow through the room wherein you sit at supper in winter, with your ealdormen and thegns, while the fire blazes in the midst and the hall is warmed, but the storms of rain and snow are raging abroad without; the sparrow, flying in at one door and immediately out at another, whilst he is within is safe from the wintry tempest; but after a short space of fair weather, he immediately vanishes out of your sight, passing from winter into winter again. So this life of man appears for a short space, but of what went before and of what is to follow we know nothing at all. If, therefore, this new doctrine contains something more certain, it justly deserves to be followed.'

The other ealdormen and counsellors, by divine inspiration, spoke to the same effect.

SAINT AUGUSTINE

CONVERSION

So was I speaking, and weeping in the most bitter contrition of my heart, when lo! I heard from a neighbouring house a voice, as of a boy or a girl, I know not, chanting and oft repeating '*Tolle, lege*; take up and read'. Instantly my countenance altered, I began to think most intently whether children were wont in any kind of play to sing such words: nor could I remember ever to have heard the like. So, checking the torrent of my tears, I arose; interpreting it to be no other than a command from God to open the book and read the first chapter I should find. For I had heard of Antony that, coming in during the reading of the Gospel, he received the admonition, as if what was being read was spoken to him: 'Go, sell all that thou hast, and give to the poor, and then shalt have treasure in heaven, and come and follow me.' And by such oracle he was forthwith converted unto Thee. Eagerly then I returned to the place where Alypius was sitting; for there had I laid the volume of the Apostle, when I arose thence. I seized, opened, and in silence read that section on which my eyes first fell: 'Not in rioting and drunkenness, not in chambering and wantonness, not in strife and envying; but put ye on the Lord Jesus Christ, and make not provision for the flesh, to fulfil the lusts thereof.' No further would I read; nor needed I: for instantly, at the end of this sentence, by a light as it were of serenity infused into my heart, all the darkness of doubt vanished away.

RICHARD ROLLE

LIKE A BIRD

When first I was converted, and became single-minded, I used to think I would be like the little bird which pines for love of its beloved, but which can rejoice in the midst of its longing when he, the loved one, comes. While it sings its joy, it is still yearning, though in sweetness and warmth. It is said that the nightingale will sing her melody all night long to please him to whom she is united. How much more ought I to sing, and as sweetly as I can, to my Jesus Christ, my soul's spouse, through the whole of this present life. Compared with the coming brightness this life is 'night', and I too languish, and languishing, faint for love. But because I faint I shall recover, and be nourished by his warmth; and I shall rejoice, and in my joy sing jubilantly the delights of love. Flute-like, I shall pour out melodious, fervent devotion, raising from the heart songs of praise to God Most High. Already they have been offered by mouth, an earnest of the praise of God, because my soul is ever avid to love; never through grief or sloth will she give up her accepted desire.

SAINT AUGUSTINE

LATE HAVE I LOVED THEE

Where then did I find Thee, that I might learn Thee? For in my memory Thou wert not, before I learned Thee. Where then did I find Thee, that I might learn Thee, but in Thyself above me? . . . Everywhere, O Truth, dost Thou give audience to all who ask counsel of Thee, and at once answerest all, though on manifold matters they ask Thy counsel. Clearly dost Thou answer, though all do not clearly hear. All consult Thee on what will, though they hear not always what they will. He is Thy best servant who looks not so much to hear that from Thee which is conformable to his own will, as rather to conform his will to what he heareth from Thee.

Too late loved I Thee, O Thou Beauty of ancient days, yet ever new! Too late I loved Thee! And behold Thou wert within, and I abroad, and there I searched for Thee; deformed as I was, running after those beauties which Thou hast made. Thou wert with me, but I was not with Thee. Things held me far from Thee - things which, unless they were in Thee, were not at all. Thou calledst and shoutedst and didst pierce my deafness. Thou flashedst and shonest and didst dispel my blindness. Thou didst send forth Thy fragrance, and I drew in breath and panted for Thee. I tasted, and still I hunger and thirst. Thou touchedst me, and I burned for Thy peace . . .

And now my whole life is in nothing but in Thine exceeding great mercy. Give what Thou commandest, and command what Thou wilt.

BLAISE PASCAL

REASON AND THE HEART

The heart has its reasons of which reason knows nothing: we know this in countless ways.

I say that it is natural for the heart to love the universal being or itself, according to its allegiance, and it hardens itself against either as it chooses. You have rejected one and kept the other. Is it reason that makes you love yourself?

It is the heart which perceives God and not the reason. That is what faith is: God perceived by the heart, not by the reason.

SIMONE WEIL

TWO LANGUAGES

A collective body is the guardian of dogma; and dogma is an object of contemplation for love, faith and intelligence, three strictly individual faculties. Hence, almost since the beginning, the individual has been ill at ease in Christianity, and this uneasiness has been notably one of the intelligence. This cannot be denied.

Christ himself who is Truth itself, when he was speaking before an assembly such as a council, did not address it in the same language as that he used in an intimate conversation with his well-beloved friend, and no doubt before the Pharisees he might easily have been accused of contradiction and error. For by one of those laws of nature which God himself respects, since he has willed them from all eternity, there are two languages which are quite distinct although made up of the same words; there is the collective language and there is the individual one. The Comforter whom Christ sends us, the Spirit of truth, speaks one or other of these languages, whichever circumstances demand, and by a necessity of their nature there is not agreement between them.

When genuine friends of God – such as was Eckhart to my way of thinking – repeat words they have heard in secret amidst the silence of the union of love, and these words are in disagreement with the teaching of the Church, it is simply that the language of the market place is not that of the nuptial chamber.

Everybody knows that really intimate conversation is only possible between two or three. As soon as there are six or seven, collective language begins to dominate. That is why it is a complete misinterpretation to apply to the Church the words 'Wheresoever two or three are gathered together in my name, there am I in the midst of them.' Christ did not say two hundred, or fifty, or ten. He said two or three. He said precisely that he always forms the third in the intimacy of the tête-à-tête.

Christ made promises to the Church, but none of these promises has the force of the expression 'Thy Father who seeth in secret.' The word of God is the secret word. He who has not heard this word, even if he adheres to all the dogmas taught by the Church, has no contact with truth.

The function of the Church as the collective keeper of dogma is indispensable. She has the right and the duty to punish those who make a clear attack upon her within the specific range of this function, by depriving them of the sacraments.

Thus, although I know practically nothing of this business, I incline to think provisionally that she was right to punish Luther.

But she is guilty of an abuse of power when she claims to force love and intelligence to model their language upon her own. This abuse of power is not of God. It comes from the natural tendency of every form of collectivism, without exception, to abuse power.

The image of the Mystical Body of Christ is very attractive. But I consider the importance given to this image to-day as one of the most serious signs of our degeneration. For our true dignity is not to be parts of a body, even though it be a mystical one, even though it be that of Christ. It consists in this, that in the state of perfection, which is the vocation of each one of us, we no longer live in ourselves, but Christ lives in us; so that through our perfection Christ in his integrity and in his indivisible unity, becomes in a sense each one of us, as he is completely in each host. The hosts are not a *part* of his body.

This present day importance of the image of the Mystical Body shows how wretchedly susceptible Christians are to outside influences. Undoubtedly there is real intoxication in being a member of the Mystical Body of Christ. But today a great many other mystical bodies, which have not Christ for their head, produce an intoxication in their members which to my way of thinking is of the same order.

As long as it is through obedience, I find sweetness in my deprivation of the joy of membership in the Mystical Body of Christ. For if God is willing to help me, I may thus bear witness that without this joy one can nevertheless be faithful to Christ unto death. Social enthusiasms have such power to-day, they raise people so effectively to the supreme degree of heroism in suffering and death, that I think it is as well that a few sheep should remain outside the fold in order to bear witness that the love of Christ is essentially something different.

GERARD MANLEY HOPKINS

THOU ART INDEED JUST LORD . . .

Justus quidem tu es, Domine, si disputem tecum; verumtamen justa loquar ad te: Quare via impiorum proseratur? Etc.

Thou art indeed just, Lord, if I contend
With thee; but, sir, so what I plead is just.
Why do sinners' ways prosper? and why must
Disappointment all I endeavour end?

Wert thou my enemy, O thou my friend,
How wouldst thou worse, I wonder, than thou dost
Defeat, thwart me? Oh, the sots and thralls of lust
Do in spare hours more thrive than I that spend,
Sir, life upon thy cause. See, banks and brakes
Now, leavèd how thick! lacèd they are again
With fretty chervil, look, and fresh wind shakes
Them; birds build – but not I build; no, but strain,
Time's eunuch, and not breed one work that wakes.
Mine, O thou lord of life, send my roots rain.

ANONYMOUS

THE PILGRIM AT ROME

To go to Rome
Is much of trouble, little of profit:
The King whom thou seekest here,
Unless thou bring Him with thee, thou wilt not find.

(TRANSLATION: KUNO MEYER)

W. H. AUDEN

ART AND RELIGION

The artist, the man who makes, is less important to mankind, for
good and evil, than the apostle, the man with a message. Without
religion, a philosophy, a code of behaviour, call it what you will,
men cannot live at all: what they believe may be absurd or revolting,
but they have to believe something. On the other hand, however
much the arts may mean to us, it is possible to imagine our lives
without them.

GERARD MANLEY HOPKINS

I WAKE AND FEEL THE FELL OF DARK . . .

I wake and feel the fell of dark, not day.
What hours, O what black hoürs we have spent
This night! what sights you, heart, saw; ways you went!
And more must, in yet longer light's delay.
With witness I speak this. But where I say
Hours I mean years, mean life. And my lament
Is cries countless, cries like dead letters sent
To dearest him that lives alas! away.

I am gall, I am heartburn. God's most deep decree
Bitter would have me taste: my taste was me;
Bones built in me, flesh filled, blood brimmed the curse.
Selfyeast of spirit a dull dough sours. I see
The lost are like this, and their scourge to be
As I am mine, their sweating selves; but worse.

JOHN HENRY NEWMAN

from *APOLOGIA PRO VITA SUA*

From the time that I became a Catholic, of course I have no further
history of my religious opinions to narrate. In saying this, I do not
mean to say that my mind has been idle, or that I have given up
thinking on theological subjects; but that I have had no variations to
record, and have had no anxiety of heart whatever. I have been in
perfect peace and contentment; I never have had one doubt. I was not
conscious to myself, on my conversion, of any change, intellectual or
moral, wrought in my mind. I was not conscious of firmer faith in the
fundamental truths of Revelation, or of more self-command; I had not
more fervour; but it was like coming into port after a rough sea; and
my happiness on that score remains to this day without interruption.

Nor had I any trouble about receiving those additional articles, which are not found in the Anglican Creed. Some of them I believed already, but not any one of them was a trial to me. I made a profession of them upon my reception with the greatest ease, and I have the same ease in believing them now. I am far of course from denying that every article of the Christian Creed, whether as held by Catholics or by Protestants, is beset with intellectual difficulties; and it is simple fact, that, for myself, I cannot answer those difficulties. Many persons are very sensitive of the difficulties of Religion; I am as sensitive of them as any one; but I have never been able to see a connection between apprehending those difficulties, however keenly, and multiplying them to any extent, and on the other hand doubting the doctrines to which they are attached. Ten thousand difficulties do not make one doubt, as I understand the subject; difficulty and doubt are incommensurate. There of course may be difficulties in the evidence; but I am speaking of difficulties intrinsic to the doctrines themselves, or to their relations with each other. A man may be annoyed that he cannot work out a mathematical problem, of which the answer is or is not given to him, without doubting that it admits of an answer, or that a certain particular answer is the true one. Of all points of faith, the being of a God is, to my own apprehension, encompassed with most difficulty, and yet borne in upon our minds with most power.

People say that the doctrine of Transubstantiation is difficult to believe; I did not believe the doctrine till I was a Catholic. I had no difficulty in believing it, as soon as I believed that the Catholic Roman Church was the oracle of God, and that she had declared this doctrine to be part of the original revelation. It is difficult, impossible, to imagine, I grant; – but how is it difficult to believe? Yet Macaulay thought it so difficult to believe, that he had need of a believer in it of talents as eminent as Sir Thomas More, before he could bring himself to conceive that the Catholics of an enlightened age could resist 'the overwhelming force of the argument against it.' 'Sir Thomas More,' he says, 'is one of the choice specimens of wisdom and virtue; and the doctrine of transubstantiation is a kind of proof charge. A faith which stands that test, will stand any test.' But for myself, I cannot indeed prove it, I cannot tell *how* it is; but I say, 'Why should it not be? What's to hinder it? What do I know of substance or matter? Just as much as the greatest philosophers, and that is nothing at all;' – so much is this the case, that there is a rising school of philosophy now, which considers phenomena to constitute the whole of our knowledge in physics. The Catholic doctrine leaves phenomena alone. It does not say that the phenomena go; on the contrary, it says that they remain;

nor does it say that the same phenomena are in several places at once. It deals with what no one on earth knows any thing about, the material substances themselves. And, in like manner, of that majestic Article of the Anglican as well as of the Catholic Creed, – the doctrine of the Trinity in Unity. What do I know of the Essence of the Divine Being? I know that my abstract idea of three is simply incompatible with my idea of one; but when I come to the question of concrete fact, I have no means of proving that there is not a sense in which one and three can equally be predicated of the Incommunicable God.

But I am going to take upon myself the responsibility of more than the mere Creed of the Church; as the parties accusing me are determined I shall do. They say, that now, in that I am a Catholic, though I may not have offences of my own against honesty to answer for, yet, at least, I am answerable for the offences of others, of my co-religionists, of my brother priests, of the Church herself. I am quite willing to accept the responsibility; and as I have been able, as I trust, by means of a few words, to dissipate, in the minds of all those who do not begin with disbelieving me, the suspicion with which so many Protestants start, in forming their judgment of Catholics, viz. that our Creed is actually set up in inevitable superstition and hypocrisy, as the original sin of Catholicism; so now I will proceed, as before, identifying myself with the Church and vindicating it, – not of course denying the enormous mass of sin and error which exists of necessity in that world-wide multiform Communion, – but going to the proof of this one point, that its system is in no sense dishonest, and that therefore the upholders and teachers of that system, as such, have a claim to be acquitted in their own persons of that odious imputation.

Starting then with the being of a God, (which, as I have said, is as certain to me as the certainty of my own existence, though when I try to put the grounds of that certainty into logical shape I find a difficulty in doing so in mood and figure to my satisfaction,) I look out of myself into the world of men, and there I see a sight which fills me with unspeakable distress. The world seems simply to give the lie to that great truth, of which my whole being is so full; and the effect upon me is, in consequence, as a matter of necessity, as confusing as if it denied that I am in existence myself. If I looked into a mirror, and did not see my face, I should have the sort of feeling which actually comes upon me, when I look into this living busy world, and see no reflexion of its Creator. This is, to me, one of those great difficulties of this absolute primary truth, to which I referred just now. Were it not for this voice, speaking so clearly in my conscience and my heart,

I should be an atheist, or a pantheist, or a polytheist when I looked into the world. I am speaking for myself only; and I am far from denying the real force of the arguments in proof of a God, drawn from the general facts of human society and the course of history, but these do not warm me or enlighten me; they do not take away the winter of my desolation, or make the buds unfold and the leaves grow within me, and my moral being rejoice. The sight of the world is nothing else than the prophet's scroll, full of 'lamentations, and mourning, and woe.'

To consider the world in its length and breadth, its various history, the many races of man, their starts, their fortunes, their mutual alienation, their conflicts; and then their ways, habits, governments, forms of worship; their enterprises, their aimless courses, their random achievements and acquirements, the important conclusion of long-standing facts, the tokens so faint and broken of a superintending design, the blind evolution of what turn out to be great powers or truths, the progress of things, as if from unreasoning elements, not towards final causes, the greatness and littleness of man, his far-reaching aims, his short duration, the curtain hung over his futurity, the disappointments of life, the defeat of good, the success of evil, physical pain, mental anguish, the prevalence and intensity of sin, the pervading idolatries, the corruptions, the dreary hopeless irreligion, that condition of the whole race, so fearfully yet exactly described in the Apostle's words, 'having no hope and without God in the world,' – all this is a vision to dizzy and appal; and inflicts upon the mind the sense of a profound mystery, which is absolutely beyond human solution.

What shall be said to this heart-piercing, reason-bewildering fact? I can only answer, that either there is no Creator, or this living society of men is in a true sense discarded from His presence. Did I see a boy of good make and mind, with the tokens on him of a refined nature, cast upon the world without provision, unable to say whence he came, his birth-place or his family connexions, I should conclude that there was some mystery connected with his history, and that he was one, of whom, from one cause or other, his parents were ashamed. Thus only should I be able to account for the contrast between the promise and the condition of his being. And so I argue about the world; – *if* there be a God, *since* there is a God, the human race is implicated in some terrible aboriginal calamity. It is out of joint with the purposes of its Creator. This is a fact, a fact as true as the fact of its existence; and thus the doctrine of what is theologically called original sin becomes to me almost as certain as that the world exists, and as the existence of God.

DOROTHY DAY

Still November. I am surprised that I am beginning to pray daily. I began because I had to. I just found myself praying. I can't get down on my knees, but I can pray while I am walking. If I get down on my knees I think, 'Do I really believe? Whom am I praying to?' And a terrible doubt comes over me, and a sense of shame, and I wonder if I am praying because I am lonely, because I am unhappy.

Then I think suddenly, scornfully, 'Here you are in a stupor of content. You are biological. Like a cow. Prayer with you is like the opiate of the people.' And over and over again in my mind that phrase is repeated jeeringly, 'Religion is the opiate of the people.'

'But,' I reason with myself, 'I am praying because I am happy, not because I am unhappy. I did not turn to God in unhappiness, in grief, in despair – to get consolation, to get something from Him.'

And encouraged that I am praying because I want to thank Him, I go on praying. No matter how dull the day, how long the walk seems, if I feel low at the beginning of the walk, the words I have been saying have insinuated themselves into my heart before I have done, so that on the trip back I neither pray nor think but am filled with exultation.

Along the beach I find it appropriate to say the Te Deum, which I learned in the Episcopal church. When I am working about the house, I find myself addressing the Blessed Virgin and turning toward her statue.

It is so hard to say how the delight in prayer has been growing on me. Two years ago, I was saying as I planted seeds in the garden, 'I *must* believe in these seeds, that they fall into the earth and grow into flowers and radishes and beans. It is a miracle to me because I do not understand it. The very fact that they use glib technical phrases does not make it any the less a miracle, and a miracle we all accept. They why not accept God's miracles?'

I am going to Mass now regularly on Sunday mornings.

SALT OF THE EARTH

SAINT MATTHEW

THE SERMON ON THE MOUNT

FROM THE *KING JAMES' BIBLE*

CHAPTER 5

And seeing the multitudes, he went up into a mountain: and when he was set, his disciples came unto him:

And he opened his mouth, and taught them, saying.

Blessed are the poor in spirit: for theirs is the kingdom of heaven.

Blessed are they that mourn: for they shall be comforted.

Blessed are the meek: for they shall inherit the earth.

Blessed are they which do hunger and thirst after righteousness: for they shall be filled.

Blessed are the merciful: for they shall obtain mercy.

Blessed are the pure in heart: for they shall see God.

Blessed are the peacemakers: for they shall be called the children of God.

Blessed are they which are persecuted for righteousness' sake: for theirs is the kingdom of heaven.

Blessed are ye, when men shall revile you, and persecute you, and shall say all manner of evil against you falsely, for my sake.

Rejoice, and be exceeding glad: for great is your reward in heaven: for so persecuted they the prophets which were before you.

Ye are the salt of the earth: but if the salt have lost his savour, wherewith shall it be salted? it is thenceforth good for nothing, but to be cast out, and to be trodden under foot of men.

Ye are the light of the world. A city that is set on an hill cannot be hid.

Neither do men light a candle, and put it under a bushel, but on a candlestick; and it giveth light unto all that are in the house.

Let your light so shine before men, that they may see your good works, and glorify your Father which is in heaven.

Think not that I am come to destroy the law, or the prophets: I am not come to destroy, but to fulfil.

For verily I say unto you, Till heaven and earth pass, one jot or one tittle shall in no wise pass from the law, till all be fulfilled.

Whosoever therefore shall break one of these least commandments, and shall teach men so, he shall be called the least in the kingdom of heaven: but whosoever shall do and teach *them*, the same shall be called great in the kingdom of heaven.

For I say unto you that except your righteousness shall exceed the righteousness of the scribes and Pharisees, ye shall in no case enter into the kingdom of heaven.

Ye have heard that it was said by them of old time, Thou shalt not kill; and whosoever shall kill shall be in danger of the judgment:

But I say unto you, That whosoever is angry with his brother without a cause shall be in danger of the judgment: and whosoever shall say to his brother, Raca, shall be in danger of the council: but whosoever shall say, Thou fool, shall be in danger of hell fire.

Therefore if thou bring thy gift to the altar, and there rememberest that thy brother hath ought against thee:

Leave there thy gift before the altar, and go thy way; first be reconciled to thy brother, and then come and offer thy gift.

Agree with thine adversary quickly, whiles thou art in the way with him; lest at any time the adversary deliver thee to the judge, and the judge deliver thee to the officer, and thou be cast into prison.

Verily I say unto thee, Thou shalt by no means come out thence, till thou hast paid the uttermost farthing.

Ye have heard that it was said by them of old time, Thou shalt not commit adultery:

But I say unto you, That whosoever looketh on a woman to lust after her hath committed adultery with her already in his heart.

And if thy right eye offend thee, pluck it out, and cast it from thee: for it is profitable for thee that one of thy members should perish and not that thy whole body should be cast into hell.

And if thy right hand offend thee, cut it off, and cast it from thee: for it is profitable for thee that one of thy members should perish and not that thy whole body should be cast into hell.

It hath been said, Whosoever shall put away his wife, let him give her a writing of divorcement:

But I say unto you, That whosoever shall put away his wife, saving for the cause of fornication, causeth her to commit adultery: and whosoever shall marry her that is divorced committeth adultery.

Again, ye have heard that it hath been said by them of old time, Thou shalt not forswear thyself, but shalt perform unto the Lord thine oaths:

But I say unto you, Swear not at all; neither by heaven; for it is God's throne:

Nor by the earth; for it is his footstool: neither by Jerusalem; for it is the city of the great King.

Neither shalt thou swear by thy head, because thou canst not make one hair white or black.

But let your communication be, Yea, yea; Nay, nay: for whatsoever is more than these cometh of evil.

Ye have heard that is hath been said, An eye for an eye, and a tooth for a tooth:

But I say unto you, That ye resist not evil: but whosoever shall smite thee on thy right check, turn to him the other also.

And if any man will sue thee at the law, and take away thy coat, let him have thy cloak also.

And whosoever shall compel thee to go a mile, go with him twain.

Give to him that asketh thee, and from him that would borrow of thee turn not thou away.

Ye have heard that it hath been said, Thou shalt love thy neighbour, and hate thine enemy.

But I say unto you, Love your enemies, bless them that curse you, do good to them that hate you, and pray for them which despitefully use you, and persecute you;

That ye may be the children of your Father which is in heaven: for he maketh his sun to rise on the evil and on the good, and sendeth rain on the just and on the unjust.

For if ye love them which love you, what reward have ye? do not even the publicans the same?

And if ye salute your brethren only, what do ye more than others? do not even the publicans so?

Be ye therefore perfect, even as your Father which is in heaven is perfect.

Take heed that ye do not your alms before men, to be seen of them: otherwise ye have no reward of your Father which is in heaven.

Therefore when thou doest thine alms, do not sound a trumpet before thee, as the hypocrites do in the synagogues and in the streets, that they may have glory of men. Verily I say unto you, They have their reward.

But when thou doest alms, let not thy left hand know what thy right hand doeth:

That thine alms may be in secret: and thy Father which seeth in secret himself shall reward thee openly.

And when thou prayest, thou shalt not be as the hyprocrites are: For they love to pray standing in the synagogues and in the corners of the streets, that they may be seen of men. Verily I say unto you, They have their reward.

But thou, when thou prayest, enter into thy closet, and when thou hast shut thy door, pray to thy Father which is in secret; and thy Father which seeth in secret shall reward thee openly.

But when ye pray, use not vain repetitions, as the heathen do: for they think that they shall be heard for their much speaking.

Be not ye therefore like unto them: for your Father knoweth what things ye have need of, before ye ask him.

After this manner therefore pray ye: Our Father which art in heaven, Hallowed be thy name.

Thy kingdom come. Thy will be done in earth, as it is in heaven.

Give us this day our daily bread.

And forgive us our debts, as we forgive our debtors.

And lead us not into temptation, but deliver us from evil: For thine is the kingdom, and the power, and the glory, for ever. Amen.

For if ye forgive men their trespasses, your heavenly Father will also forgive you:

But if ye forgive not men their trespasses, neither will your father forgive your trespasses.

Moreover when ye fast, be not, as the hypocrites, of a sad countenance: for they disfigure their faces, that they may appear unto men to fast. Verily I say unto you, They have their reward.

But thou, when thou fastest, anoint thine head, and wash thy face;

That thou appear not unto men to fast, but unto thy Father which is in secret: and thy Father, which seeth in secret, shall reward thee openly.

Lay not up for yourselves treasures upon earth, where moth and rust doth corrupt, and where thieves break through and steal:

But lay up for yourselves treasures in heaven, where neither moth nor rust doth corrupt, and where thieves do not break through nor steal:

For where your treasure is, there will your heart be also.

The light of the body is the eye: if therefore thine eye be single, thy whole body shall be full of light.

But if thine eye be evil, thy whole body shall be full of darkness. If therefore the light that is in thee be darkness, how great is that darkness!

No man can serve two masters: for either he will hate the one, and love the other; or else he will hold to the one, and despise the other. Ye cannot serve God and mammon.

Therefore I say unto you, Take no thought for your life, what ye shall eat, or what ye shall drink: nor yet for your body, what ye shall put on. Is not the life more than meat, and the body than raiment?

Behold the fowls of the air: for they sow not, neither do they reap, nor gather into barns: yet your heavenly Father feedeth them. Are ye not much better than they?

Which of you by taking thought can add one cubit unto his stature?

And why take ye thought for raiment? Consider the lilies of the field, how they grow; they toil not, neither do they spin:

And yet I say unto you, That even Solomon in all his glory was not arrayed like one of these.

Wherefore, if God so clothe the grass of the field, which to day is, and to morrow is cast into the oven, shall he not much more clothe you, O ye of little faith?

Therefore take no thought, saying, What shall we eat? or, What shall we drink? or, Wherewithal shall we be clothed?

(For after all these things do the Gentiles seek:) for your heavenly Father knoweth that ye have need of all these things.

But seek ye first the kingdom of God, and his righteousness; and all these things shall be added unto you.

Take therefore no thought for the morrow: for the morrow shall take thought for the things of itself. Sufficient unto the day is the evil thereof.

CHAPTER 7

Judge not, that ye be not judged.

For with what judgment ye judge, ye shall be judged: and with what measure ye mete, it shall be measured to you again.

And why beholdest thou the mote that is in thy brother's eye, but considerest not the beam that is in thine own eye?

Or how wilt thou say to thy brother, Let me pull out the mote out of thine eye; and, behold, a beam is in thine own eye?

Thou hypocrite, first cast out the beam out of thine own eye: and then shalt thou see clearly to cast out the mote out of thy brother's eye.

Give not that which is holy unto the dogs, neither cast ye your pearls before swine, lest they trample them under their feet, and turn again and rend you.

Ask, and it shall be given you; seek, and ye shall find; knock, and it shall be opened unto you:

For every one that asketh receiveth; and he that seeketh findeth; and to him that knocketh it shall be opened.

Or what man is there of you, whom if his son ask bread, will he give him a stone?

Or if he ask a fish, will he give him a serpent?

If ye then, being evil, know how to give good gifts unto your children, how much more shall your Father which is in heaven give good things to them that ask him?

Therefore all things whatsoever ye would that men should do to you, do ye even so to them: for this is the law and the prophets.

Enter ye in at the strait gate: for wide is the gate, and broad is the way, that leadeth to destruction, and many there be which go in thereat:

Because strait is the gate, and narrow is the way, which leadeth unto life, and few there be that find it.

Beware of false prophets, which come to you in sheep's clothing, but inwardly they are ravening wolves.

Ye shall know them by their fruits. Do men gather grapes of thorns, or figs of thistles?

Even so every good tree bringeth forth good fruit; but a corrupt tree bringeth forth evil fruit.

A good tree cannot bring forth evil fruit, neither can a corrupt tree bring forth good fruit.

Every tree that bringeth not forth good fruit is hewn down, and cast into the fire.

Wherefore by their fruits ye shall know them.

Not every one that saith unto me, Lord, Lord, shall enter into the kingdom of heaven; but he that doeth the will of my Father which is in heaven.

Many will say to me in that day, Lord, Lord, have we not prophesied in thy name? and in thy name have cast out devils? and in thy name done many wonderful works?

And then will I profess unto them, I never knew you: depart from me, ye that work iniquity.

Therefore whosoever heareth these sayings of mine, and doeth them, I will liken him unto a wise man, which built his house upon a rock:

And the rain descended, and the floods came, and the winds blew, and beat upon that house; and it fell not: for it was founded upon a rock.

And every one that heareth these sayings of mine, and doeth them not, shall be likened unto a foolish man, which built his house upon the sand:

And the rain descended, and the floods came, and the winds blew, and beat upon that house: and it fell: and great was the fall of it.

And it came to pass, when Jesus had ended these sayings, the people were astonished at his doctrine:

For he taught them as one having authority, and not as the scribes.

SAINT JOHN OF THE CROSS

It was not from want of will that I have refrained from writing to you, for truly do I wish you all good; but because it seemed to me that enough has been said already to effect all that is needful, and that what is wanting (if indeed anything be wanting) is not writing or speaking - whereof ordinarily there is more than enough - but silence and work. For whereas speaking distracts, silence and work collect thoughts and strengthen the spirit. As soon therefore as a person understands what has been said to him for his good, there is no further need to hear or to discuss; but to set himself in earnest to practise what he has leaned with silence and attention, in humility, charity and contempt of self.

LEONARDO BOFF

SAINT FRANCIS AND THE POOR

One day, the blessed Francis, near the Church of Saint Mary of the angels, called to Brother Leo and said to him: 'Brother Leo, write this down.'

Leo answered: 'I am ready.'

'Write down, what perfect joy is,' Francis continued.

'A messenger from Paris arrives and says that all of the teachers at the university want to enter the order. Write: that is not perfect joy. And though all of the prelates beyond the Alps, archbishops and bishops, and even the very kings of England and France were to enter the order, write: that is not perfect joy. And if you were to receive news that all our brothers went to preach to the infidels and converted them all to the faith, or that I received so much grace from God that I cure the sick and do many miracles: I assure you that that is not perfect joy.'

'What, then, is perfect joy?' asked Brother Leo.

'Imagine,' Francis continued, 'that I return to Perugia on the darkest of nights, a night so cold that everything is covered with snow, and icicles form in the folds of my habit, hitting my legs and making them bleed. Shrouded in snow and shivering with cold, I arrive at the door of the friary, and after calling out for a long time, the brother porter gets up and asks: 'Who is it?' And I respond: 'It is I, Brother Francis.' The porter says: 'Be on your way. Now is not the time to arrive at a friary. I will not open the door for you.' I insist and he answers: 'Be on your way right now. You are stupid and an idiot. We are already many here and we do not need you.' I insist once more: 'For the love of God, let me in, just for tonight.' And he answers: 'Not even to talk. Go to the leper colony that is nearby.'

'Well, Brother Leo, if after all this, I do not lose patience and remain calm, believe me, that is perfect joy, true virtue, and the salvation of my soul.'

The radical poverty lived by Francis in solidarity with the poor and in following of the poor Christ gives us the opportunity to reflect on the characteristics of liberation that arise from that attitude, and on the contributions of his practice to the global process of the emancipation of the oppressed of our day. Christian reflection during the last decade developed what we call the theology of liberation, which implies a vigorous articulation of the discourse of faith with the discourse of society, on the level of Christian effectiveness in terms of the liberation of the poor who, in the Latin American continent, represent the vast majority of the people, both Christian and oppressed.

The theme of liberation is not new, though it certainly is the strongest impulse in modern culture. Generally, we can state that the history of the past five centuries centres in large part on the process of emancipation. The first significant emergence came with Galileo Galilei and the liberation of *reason* from within the religious totality that impeded the free flight of thought in the discovery of the working mechanisms of the world. Then, there was the liberation of the *citizen* from the absolutism of the kings, to see the citizen as the real bearer and delegate of political powers, as Rouseau thought. With his writings, there was the liberation of *spirit* alienated in physical matter by way of the transfiguration of absolute Spirit. With Marx, attention turned to the liberation of the *proletariat* from capitalist economic domination with the aim of arriving at a socialist society without class distinctions. With Nietzsche, there was the liberation of *life*, shortened and suffocated by the sophistication of metaphysics, morals, culture. Freud developed a whole plan for the liberation of the *psyche* from its interior bonds (neurosis, psychosis, etc.). Marcuse launched the manifesto of the liberation of *industrial man*, reduced to only one dimension by assembly-line production. The worldwide feminist movement promotes the liberation of *women*, faced with a patriarchal and male culture, toward a less sexist and more personalistic society.

All modern revolutions promoted and promote the widening of the sphere of human liberation: the scientific revolution, the bourgeois revolution, the socialist revolution, the atomic revolution, and the cybernetic revolution.

We can see that this whole emancipatory process is done behind the Church's back, beside it, or against it. The contribution of Christian-Catholics was minimal. However, the Judeo-Christian influence is not absent from all these movements. Some of the distinguished representatives of modern liberation were Jews: Marx, Nietzsche, Jung, Marcuse, Einstein. They carried with them the liberating wisdom of the Old Testament prophets and the sense that history continually should be made to be worthy of the Creator.

Liberation theology is understood in the thread of these great movements of emancipation that characterise the modern age. It was born on the periphery of the world and the Church, in Latin America, and is spreading to Africa and Asia, where the poor see in it the articulated voice of their poverty, which demands liberation. It may be the only time, in the last few centuries, that faith has proposed to be a concrete factor in the liberation of the oppressed in a conscious and planned way.

At the base of this theology of the poor there is a spiritual experience of protest and love. Above all, it is a holy ire, the very virtue of the prophets, against the collective misery of the poor. With the words of Paul VI in *Evangelii Nuntiandi*, taken up by the bishops of Puebla: 'want, chronic and endemic illnesses, illiteracy, poverty, injustices in international relations and especially in commercial interchanges, situations of economic and cultural neocolonialism sometimes as cruel as former political colonialism' (nos. 30,26). This reality does not please God, because it humiliates His children. It needs to be changed. Second, underlying the theology of liberation is a committed love that translates into the preferential and solidary option for the poor.

SAINT CLARE OF ASSISI

CARING FOR THE SICK

Regarding the sisters who are ill, the Abbess is strictly bound to require with all solicitude by herself and through other sisters what these sick sisters may need both by way of counsel and of food and other necessities and, according to the resources of the place, she is to provide for them charitably and kindly. This is to be done because all are obliged to serve and provide for their sisters who are ill just as they would wish to be served themselves if they were suffering from any infirmity. Each should make known her needs to the other with confidence. For if a mother loves and nourishes her daughter according to the flesh, how much more loving must a sister love and nourish her sister according to the Spirit.

Those who are ill may lie on sackcloth filled with straw and may use feather pillows for their head; and those who need woollen stockings and quilts may use them.

JEAN VANIER

SERVING THE HANDICAPPED

In 1963, while I was teaching philosophy at the University of Toronto, I visited France, where I went to see Father Thomas Philippe, a Dominican priest whom I had met some years earlier. At that time, Father Thomas was chaplain to a Residence for thirty men with a mental handicap in Trosly-Breuil. It was the first time in my life (I was thirty-five) that I had met people with a mental handicap. I was amazed and bewildered, and somehow a little overwhelmed. The cry of anger in those men, their deep sadness and at the same time their incredible cry for relationship, moved me.

These men seemed so different from my students at the University who seemed only interested in my head and in what they could get out of it in order to pass their exams, but were not at all concerned by my person. These people I met in Trosly could not care less about what was in my head; they were interested in my person. It was obvious that they craved friendship, a relationship where they would be seen as unique. Somehow their cry evoked something deep within me. But at the same time I was overwhelmed by their needs.

That is how I became interested in the plight of these people, and I began visiting asylums and hospitals. I saw many men and women living in crowded and most unbearable situations.

And so it was that a few months later I bought a house in Trosly, and invited two men to come and live with me. Both had mental handicaps; neither had any family as their parents had died. They had been put into a rather dismal institution. We started living together in a small rather dilapidated house. We began to discover each other. They had their anger and fears, but also their hopes. I too had my anger and fears, but also my hopes. Little by little I discovered the immense pain hidden inside the loneliness they felt, their broken self-image, because they had been pushed around so much in life and had received so little respect. I also came to know their incredible goodness.

Other people came to help, and so we were able to welcome more handicapped people. My idea was to create a little 'home', a little family, for those who had no 'home', no family. I did not want l'Arche (the name given to the first home) to be an institution, but a community where each person had his or her place, where we could work, grow, celebrate and pray together.

The French government recognised us quite quickly. It was in need of places to welcome people with mental handicaps. We were thus able to buy another home in the village, and little by little we grew. There are now some four hundred people in our community, in many small homes scattered throughout Trosly and the neighbouring villages. Each home is as independent as possible.

Other people from other countries come to visit or to live with us for a while. Some were deeply touched by their experience here and in union with us they began to found similar communities in their own country. Now in 1985, there are seventy communities in sixteen different countries. We have a little community near Ouagadougou in Burkina Faso where we have welcomed four children who had been abandoned. We have started a school for them and for some of the handicapped children in the area. There is a community in one of the slum areas of Tegucigalpa in Honduras, where we are trying to serve the needs of handicapped people there.

In the centre of Calcutta we were given a house and the basement of a church for a workshop. We have communities in Scotland and Ireland. In England there are four communities, in London, Bognor Regis, Liverpool and near Canterbury. Each one is inspired by the same spirit and lives off the same principle: to create community with people who have a mental handicap. All these communities are grouped together in a rather loose-knit federation, and all the communities are part of the larger family of l'Arche.

The inspiration at the basis of each community is religious, but the ways of expressing the love of God may be different. I myself am Roman Catholic and the first community of l'Arche in Trosly was inspired by my faith and by the faith of Father Thomas Philippe. We wanted the community to be a place of love and hope, a place of sharing, a place where people could find peace of heart and forgiveness. We wanted l'Arche to be a place where the poorer person was at the centre rather than the 'helpers'. In England our communities welcome predominantly Christians from the Anglican tradition. Very quickly our homes there became ecumenical. In India our communities are essentially made up of Hindus, Moslems and Christians. Yes, our differences are sometimes painful, but we are learning that the poor can call us to unity.

Many things happen in our communities. There are crises of all sorts. Some people need good psychological help; some take a long time to find any peace of heart or healing. Some like to work, others hate it. There is joy, there is pain; it is the joy and the pain of living together.

Most of the people we welcome are called to be with us all their lives but this depends, of course, on the gravity of their handicap. A few leave and get married. But the majority are much too severely wounded. Assistants come for periods of one or two years, and more and more are putting their roots down in community, making a life commitment to the family. This, of course, is essential. There are so many people in institutions or living more independently in apartments, but who are yearning for a network of friendship, a community life. They have contact with professionals who are prepared to work with them and who do a magnificent job. But there are few people in society willing to climb down the ladder of success and to become a brother or a sister to a person with a mental handicap.

It is true that sometimes it is very taxing to live with people in deep anguish and stress. Experience at l'Arche has shown us that it is also important to care for the carers. Assistants too need to be supported and helped in many ways, particularly if they are called to put their roots down and to stay the rest of their life in a community. With twenty years' experience we now see clearly that they can only do this if they discover that the person with a handicap is a source of life and strength for them; if they themselves are not there just to 'do good' to another but also to receive something from her or him; that they too are called to live in community and to be nourished by those who are at the heart of the community.

Our society frequently sees the world in the form of a ladder: there is a bottom and a top. Everything and everyone encourages us to climb up that ladder, to seek success, promotions, wealth and power. At l'Arche, in living with our wounded brothers and sisters, we are discovering that if we are to live humanely, it is not the ladder that we should take as a model, but rather a living body. In a body there are many different parts: each one is important, even the smallest and the weakest. No one part can say it is the best and that it does not need the others. Each part is made so that the whole body can function well. In the body, even the weakest members know they are needed and important.

People with a mental handicap who come to our communities are called to rise up in hope and to discover the beauty of their beings and their capacities, no matter how limited these may be. Those who come to help are called to what is most beautiful in their own hearts: the capacity to be present to give life, through their love, to those in distress. And thus the body is formed. We discover we are linked together.

Because we are linked together we learn to forgive each other, for we can so easily hurt one another when we live together. We learn to celebrate the fact that we have been called together. Little by little we become people of joy because we are people of prayer, people within a covenanted relationship.

DOROTHY DAY

A BRIEF SOJOURN IN JAIL

July 30. We left Kennedy Airport at noon for San Francisco, Eileen Egan and I. She was attending, as I, too, was supposed to, the 50th Anniversary of the War Resisters League. Joan Baez had invited me to be at her Institute for the Study of Nonviolence for the week with some members of Cesar Chavez's United Farm Workers' Union. When we arrived, the plans had changed because of the mass arrests of farm workers for defying an injunction against mass picketing in Kern County. There was now a strike in the vineyards, as well as the lettuce fields, because the growers would not renew their contracts with the farm workers and were instead making new contracts with the Teamsters.

The strike was widespread and mass arrests were continuing. My path was clear: the UFW has everything that belongs to a new social order. Since I had come to picket where an injunction was prohibiting picketing, it appeared that I would spend my weeks in California in jail, not at conferences.

July 31. A very hot drive down the valley to Delano, arriving as the strike meeting ended. Today many Jesuits were arrested. Also Sisters who had been attending a conference in San Francisco. Mass in the evening at Bakersfield ended a tremendous demonstration, flag-carrying Mexicans, singing, chanting, marching. When the Mass began there were so many people that it was impossible to kneel, but there was utter silence.

August 1. Up to 2 a.m., picketed all day, covering many vineyards. Impressive lines of police, all armed – clubs and guns. We talked to them, pleaded with them to lay down their weapons. One was black. His mouth twitched as he indicated that, no, he did not enjoy being there. Two other police came and walked away with him. I told the other police I would come back the next day and read the Sermon on the Mount to them. I was glad I had my folding chair-cane so I could rest occasionally during picketing, and sit there before the police to talk to them. I had seen a man that morning sitting at the entrance to workers' shacks with a rifle across his knees.

August 2. Slept at Sanger with nurses from one of the farm workers' clinics. Up at 4 a.m., was at the park before dawn. Cesar came and spoke to us abut the injunction and arrests (wonder when he sleeps?) and we set out in cars to picket the area where big and small growers had united to get the injunction. Three white police buses arrived some time later and we were warned that we were to disperse. When we refused we were ushered into the buses and brought to this 'industrial farm' (which they do not like us to call a jail or prison, though we are under lock and key and our barracks surrounded by barbed wire). Here we are, ninety-nine women and fifty men, including thirty Sisters and two priests.

August 3. Maria Hernandez got ill in the night. Taken to Fresno Hospital, cardiograph taken, and she was put in the Fresno jail. (She was returned to us still ill August 7. She worries about her children.) Another Mexican mother in our barracks has ten children and there certainly was a crowd visiting her. Such happy, beautiful families – it reminded me of the tribute paid to the early Christians when they were imprisoned and the hordes of their fellow Christians visited them, and made a great impression on their guards.

I must copy down the charges made against me (we were listed in groups of ten): 'The said defendants, on or about August 2, were persons remaining present at the place of a riot, rout and unlawful assembly, who did willfully and unlawfully fail, refuse and neglect after the same had been lawfully warned to disperse.'

Some of the other women listed in the criminal complaint in my group of ten were Demetria Landavazo de Leon, Maria de Jesus Ochoa, Efigenia Garcia de Rojas, Esperanza Alanis de Perales. How I wish I could list them all.

During crucial meetings between Cesar Chavez and the Teamsters the Sisters all signed up for a night of prayer, taking two-hour shifts all through the night, while the Mexican woman all knelt along the tables in the centre and prayed the rosary together. Barracks A, B, and D were alive with prayer.

Tonight a young Mexican legal assistant of the union was brutally and contemptuously ordered out when he attempted to talk to us. There were only three incidents I could have complained of: another case of rudeness, and the attempt to search the bodies of the prisoners for food smuggled in.

Today I had interesting conversation with Jo von Gottfried, a teacher of rhetoric in Berkeley, a great lover of St Thomas and St Augustine. I tried to understand what 'rhetoric' really means and she explained, but I cannot remember now.

August 8. Today Joan Baez, her mother, and Daniel Ellsberg visited us. Joan sang to us and the other prisoners in the yard. There was a most poignant prison song. It tore at your heart. She was singing when other prisoners were being brought to the dining room and she turned her back to us and sang to all of them directly, as they stopped their line to listen.

Daniel Ellsberg said Cesar Chavez, the thought of him, had given him courage during his two-year ordeal in the courts.

August 9. I'm all mixed up in my dates. Dr Evan Thomas came today, ninety-one and tall, lean, strong-looking. God bless him. And Father Don Hessler, whom we've known since he was a seminarian at Maryknoll. He suffered years of imprisonment under the Japanese in World War II.

August 11. Good talks with Sister Felicia and Sister Timothy of Barracks B, who are good spokeswomen for our group. Two writers from *Newsweek* called. They were interested in 'the religious slant' of the strike.

August 12. Union lawyers visiting us say we'll be free tomorrow. A peaceful Sunday. Mass in the evening. Today the Mexican girls were singing and clapping and teaching the Sisters some Mexican dancing. They reminded me of St Teresa of Avila playing her castanets at recreation.

August 13. We packed our bags last night and a first busload, including me, left our farm labour camp this morning, reached the jail, and were turned back! We then spent hours in the 'rec' hall, where a team of 'public defenders,' whom we were supposed to have seen Sunday, sat around (perhaps I saw *one* working), while Sister Felicia interviewed all the women in our barracks for the rest of the day and filled out the forms which the judge required.

In the evening we were all finally loaded in vans and brought to Fresno, where, with a great crowd in the park in front of the courthouse, we celebrated Mass.

* * *

There is still no contract signed by grape growers with the union. Instead, there have been two deaths, that of Naji Daifullah, an Arab striker from Yemen, and Juan de la Cruz of Delano. We attended the funeral service of Naji at Forty Acres. A mile-long parade of marchers walked the four miles in a broiling sun from Delano with black flags, black armbands, and ribbons, and stood through the long service while psalms from the Office of the Dead were heard clearly over loudspeakers and the words from the Book of Wisdom: 'In the sight of the unwise they seemed to die but they are at peace.' There were Moslem chants as well. Five hundred Arabs recently came here from Yemen – to this land of opportunity – and one has met with death, his skull fractured by a deputy wielding a heavy flashlight.

Juan de la Cruz was shot in the chest. His funeral Mass was offered by Bishop Arzube of Los Angeles. Two men have shed their blood. Cesar Chavez has requested a three-day fast and a renewed zeal in boycotting lettuce and grapes. There is no money left in the treasury of the union, especially after death benefits have been paid to the families of the dead strikers. One of the Mexican girls in jail told me proudly that their $3.50 dues paid benefits for lives born and lives lost. And there were all the clinics operating at Calexico, Delano, Sanger, and other places. The Farm Workers' Union is a community to be proud of, and would that all our unions might become a 'community of communities.'

I must mention a prayer I wrote in the front of my New Testament, and hope our readers, while they read, say this for the strikers:

Dear Pope John – please, yourself a *campesino*, watch over the United Farm Workers. Raise up more and more leader-servants throughout the country to stand with Cesar Chavez in this nonviolent struggle with Mammon, in all the rural districts of North and South, in the cotton fields, beet fields, potato fields, in our orchards and vineyards, our orange groves – wherever men, women, and children work on the land. Help make a new order wherein justice flourishes, and, as Peter Maurin, himself a peasant, said so simply, 'where it is easier to be good.'

September 1973

MARGARET HEBBLETHWAITE

MARY OF MAGDALA

We women grew very close in those days, as we huddled together for courage. Hand in hand, or arm in arm, we followed him now in silence – I and the other Mary, Joanna and Susanna and Salome. Gone were the Galilean days of confident ministry and happy partnership. I felt all activity, all thought, all planning, all initiative was drained out of me, and I had strength only to trail behind, borne along by the support of my sisters in the gospel.

Together we walked behind him over the cobbles, like a sad and subdued royal retinue, as he entered Jerusalem on the back of a donkey, while the crowd bayed, 'Blessed is the king who comes in the name of God.' Our hearts were turning over with fear and trepidation, while the people shouted and whooped for joy. Jesus wept with anguish, and we were close enough to hear him cry, 'If only you had recognised on this day the things that make for peace.'

Together we walked behind him up the steps to the temple, and meekly watched him overthrowing tables and chairs and yelling at the stall-holders that they had turned God's house of prayer into a den of thieves. Jesus threw himself about this way and that, banging and arguing, as we stood to the side like a bunch of stupid dummies. then together we turned and followed him out again.

Together we returned to the temple and stood at his side as we heard him preaching against the priests and elders. He told them that prostitutes would go to heaven before them. He likened them to murderers, who set upon their landlord's only son and killed him. And he told them they were like a man at a wedding feast who had not bothered to dress for the occasion: he would be bound hand and foot and thrown into the outer darkness, where there was weeping and gnashing of teeth. The Pharisees and elders were white with anger. Each time we went into the temple we were afraid we would not emerge again safely.

Joanna was a help on those occasions, for her experience in Herod's court had given her self-confidence that made her walk tall and free. Salome was another support: as a mother of two adult sons who were among the twelve, her commitment to Jesus was very solid. And the other Mary was the one who most often put her arm around me to give me courage. And so we bore each other up.

GEORGE ELIOT

PRELUDE

Who that cares much to know the history of man, and how the mysterious mixture behaves under the varying experiments of Time, has not dwelt, at least briefly, on the life of Saint Theresa, has not smiled with some gentleness at the thought of the little girl walking forth one morning hand-in-hand with her still smaller brother, to go and seek martyrdom in the country of the Moors? Out they toddled from rugged Avila, wide-eyed and helpless-looking as two fawns, but with human hearts, already beating to a national idea; until domestic reality met them in the shape of uncles, and turned them back from their great resolve. That child-pilgrimage was a fit beginning. Theresa's passionate, ideal nature demanded an epic life: what were many-volumed romances of chivalry and the social conquests of a brilliant girl to her? Her flame quickly burned up that light fuel; and, fed from within, soared after some illimitable satisfaction, some object which would never justify wariness, which would reconcile self-despair, with the rapturous consciousness of life beyond self. She found her epos in the reform of a religious order.

That Spanish woman who lived three hundred years ago was certainly not the last of her kind. Many Theresas have been born who found for themselves no epic life wherein there was a constant unfolding of far-resonant action; perhaps only a life of mistakes, the offspring of a certain spiritual grandeur ill-matched with the meanness of opportunity; perhaps a tragic failure which found no sacred poet and sank unwept into oblivion. With dim lights and tangled circumstance they tried to shape their thought and deed in noble agreement; but after all, to common eyes their struggles seemed mere inconsistency and formlessness: for these later-born Theresas were helped by no coherent social faith and order which could perform the function of knowledge for the ardently willing soul. Their ardour alternated between a vague ideal and the common yearning of womanhood; so that the one was disapproved as extravagance, and the other condemned as a lapse.

Some have felt that these blundering lives are due to the inconvenient indefiniteness with which the Supreme Power has fashioned the natures of women: if there were one level of feminine incompetence as strict as the ability to count three and no more, the social lot of women might be treated with scientific certitude. Meanwhile the indefiniteness remains, and the limits of variation are really much wider than any one would imagine from the sameness of women's coiffure and the favourite love-stories in prose and verse. Here and there a cygnet is reared uneasily among the ducklings in the brown pond, and never finds the living stream in fellowship with its own oary-footed kind. Here and there is born a Saint Theresa, foundress of nothing, whose loving heart-beats and sobs after an unattained goodness tremble off and are dispersed among hindrances, instead of centering in some long-recognisable deed.

KATE O'BRIEN

SAINT TERESA OF AVILA

The great, the illuminated, the chosen ones, even while they are of our flesh and to that extent share our dangers and humiliations, yet so translate those threats, so dazzlingly purify them that they are not to be interpreted by our poor rushlights of surmise. Teresa was made of flesh like us, and that it plagued and wearied her – in youth, through its energetic, natural storms, and in maturity and age through its infirm, sick drag on her spirit – we know. But after that? We can read her indeed, and learn and wonder – but what comment dare we make on a fellow creature who has sped so far while seeming to stay with us? Crashaw can snatch great phrases for Teresa's 'draughts of intellectual day', but she escapes him, as, the more one reads her, the more one understands she must escape us all. Probably it was all that she desired to do, apart from pleasing 'His Majesty' and doing what He told her.

Yet the human charm persists, and we persist in twisting it over and puzzling at it; because its humanity relates the great one to us, and that is not only flattering but also consoling.

Teresa was a saint. She was alarming, she was, if you like, deluded; she was, if you like, mad. But she accomplished a great deal, speaking mundanely; she wrote with sanity, beauty and modesty, about high and dangerous matters; she charmed almost everyone she ever met; she was gay, tender and witty in her letters and in all her writings, and she was as much impeded by small faults and vanities as any saint dare be – as well she knew. So, however far beyond us she extended here on earth, she still is ours and dear to us, in a large part of her records. She was indeed Teresa of Jesus, as 'His Majesty' told her; but still somehow we cling to her in hope. She was once a sinner, as she is never tired of telling us; she was always a wit and an observer; she loved her brothers and her friends. Dangerous as her territory may be we do not find it barren of the flowers we know. The trouble really is that, incomprehensible as she may finally be, no sane person can read Teresa without liking her. The charm lives with the sanctity, the wit with the vision, the human simplicity with the ineffable raptures.

'You must forgive me,' she would write to a friend she had hurt. 'With those I love I am insufferable, so anxious am I to have them perfect in everything.'

To 'His Majesty' she often complained of His harsh treatment. Once, when He had tried her almost past her strength she grumbled very firmly, and heard Him reply: 'Teresa, this is how I treat My friends.' 'Which is why You have so few,' said she.

On another occasion she was importuning Him unmercifully, night and day, in regard to the insuperable-seeming difficulties of her Burgos foundation – when she heard Him say: 'I have heard you, daughter. Please leave Me alone.' Whereat, she records, she was as much delighted and reassured as if the convent was already happily established. (She had an endearing way of reporting 'His Majesty' as if He spoke very much in her own forthright style.)

To find the full charm of her one must read her letters – to her prioresses, to Gracián, to her spiritual directors. 'I laughed at what you told me . . .' ' . . . Ah, how I have been amused!' And when she has narrated some comedy or quoted some light poem of her own: 'God forgive you,' she writes, 'for making me waste my time like this!'

She was nimble at occasional verse, and vain of her skill in this *genre*. Among her many attempts none is more amusing than the hymn she wrote for her community when they were afraid that their new, poor habits, of very coarse frieze, were likely to attract and harbour vermin.

Since Thou givest us, King of Heaven,
New clothes like these,
Do Thou keep all nasty creatures
Out of this frieze.
Daughters, you've the Cross upon you;
Have courage too.
Since salvation He has won you,
He'll bring you through.
He'll direct you, He'll defend you,
If Him you please.
All: *Do Thou keep all nasty creatures*
Out of this frieze!

There are more verses, with the same refrain. Teresa and her nuns at St Joseph's, Avila, sang this composition in choir on the first day of their anxiety about the new habits – which shows that life was not without gaiety in her houses. Indeed it was not. She had a resounding way with ordinary life. We have all surely heard her famous claim for commonplace labours: *Entre los pucheros anda el Señor*. 'The Lord walks among the saucepans.'

She was brilliant herself among the saucepans – the best cook in the Order, her contemporaries said. And an undaunted scrubber of floors and washer and mender of clothes. A full and ordinary human being, in fact; one actively and truly with her fellows, though always ahead of them too, and by an accident in regard to which she was always reticent, above them.

LADY GREGORY

SAINT BRIGIT FILLS THE VESSELS

One time the serving boy went to the druid's house, and they asked was the girl minding the dairy well. And he said 'I am thankful, and the calves are fat;' for he dared not say anything against the girl, and she not there. But the druid got word of what she was doing, and he came to visit the farm, and his wife along with him; and the cows were doing well, and the calves were fat. Then they went into the dairy, having with them a vessel eighteen hands in height. And Brigit bade them welcome and washed their feet, and made ready food for them, and after that they bade her fill up the vessel with butter. And she had but a churning and a half for them, and she went into the kitchen where it was stored and it is what she said:

'O my High Prince who can do all these things, this is not a forbidden asking; bless my kitchen with thy right hand!

'My kitchen, the kitchen of the white Lord; a kitchen that was blessed by my King; a kitchen where there is butter.

'My Friend is coming, the son of Mary; it is he blessed my kitchen; the Prince of the world comes to this place; that there may be plenty with him!' After she had made that hymn she brought the half of the churning from the place where it was stored; and the druid's wife mocked at her and said 'It is good filling for a large vessel this much is!' 'Fill your vessel' said Brigit, 'and God will add something to it.' And she was going back to her kitchen and bringing half a churning every time and saying every time a verse of those verses. And if all the vessels of the men of Munster had been brought to her she would have filled the whole of them.

LADY GREGORY

THE DRYING OF BRIGIT'S CLOAK

One time Brennain, saint of the Gael, came from the west to Brigit, to the plain of the Lífé, for he wondered at the great name she had for doing miracles and wonders. And Brigit came in from her sheep to welcome him, and as she came into the house she laid her cloak that was wet on the rays of the sun, and they held it up the same as hooks. Then Brennain bade his serving lad to put his cloak on the sun rays in the same way, and he put it on them, but twice it fell from them. Then Brennain himself put it on them the third time, and there was anger on him, and that time it stopped on the rays.

LADY GREGORY

THE THINGS BRIGIT WISHED FOR

These were the wishes of Brigit:

'I would wish a great lake of ale for the King of Kings; I would wish the family of Heaven to be drinking it through life and time.

'I would wish the men of Heaven in my own house; I would wish vessels of peace to be giving to them.

'I would wish vessels full of alms to be giving away; I would wish ridges of mercy for peace-making.

'I would wish joy to be in their drinking: I would wish Jesus to be here among them.

'I would wish the three Marys of great name; I would wish the people of Heaven from every side.

'I would wish to be a rent-payer to the Prince; the way if I was in trouble he would give me a good blessing.'

Whatever, now, Brigit would ask of the Lord, he would give it to her on the moment. And it is what her desire was, to satisfy the poor, to banish every hardship, and to save every sorrowful man.

GERARD MANLEY HOPKINS

HEAVEN-HAVEN

A nun takes the veil

I have desired to go
    Where springs not fail,
To fields where flies no sharp and sided hail
    And a few lilies blow.

And I have asked to be
    Where no storms come,
Where the green swell is in the havens dumb,
    And out of the swing of the sea.

MARY LOUDON

AN INTERVIEW WITH FELICITY (A POOR CLARE NUN)

You could argue that we miss out, but then I don't have to go to the Downs to see the beauty of God's creation. I'd certainly see another aspect of it there but then I haven't seen Niagara Falls either. I mean, am I lacking as a person because I haven't seen Niagara Falls? And equally, coming back to this economy of love, I am loving the people around me. It's not the *number* of people I love, it's the amount of love I love with that is important. We, as part of the human race, are taking time apart, and if you see us as part of the human race as a whole, then it is a tiny bit of time that is being given to God.

However, when I came here a lot of people talked as if I was embarking on a higher type of life, but it's not, it's just different. I don't think the apostolic and the contemplative life can be compared, I think they're two faces of the same coin. And it's actually the main reason I agreed to work with you, because it's something I feel very strongly about, and I feel is misunderstood.

You know, it's not a case of the worker bees and the drones, or even the worker bees and the queen bee. We're all workers: we just happen to be working in different ways. It's better for me to be here than elsewhere, that's all.

Still, many people find this kind of life practically impossible to accept. I suspect that as human beings what we don't understand we tend to write off, simply because it's easier to handle things like that, and a way of life that is radically different questions people. And they can either stand and face the question or else they can say, 'Nuns: they're mad.' And it's often easier to say, 'They're mad.' But people can be totally different and still be absolutely sane! It is possible to say: 'I don't understand you, but I accept you. I don't understand what you're doing but I can see it's obviously got a value because of what it's making you.'

Some people might feel sort of jealous of my conviction, that I know what I want, where I'm going. But then, they haven't seen all the convolutions that have gone on inside me. You know? Conviction isn't there all the time. It can be removed for anybody. Even Christ on the cross cried out, 'My God, my God, why have you forsaken me?' and he *meant* that, I mean it wasn't just a pious quotation then. He experienced the feeling that God wasn't there, that God was *not*. And I suspect we all have to experience that because the meaning of faith is 'believing without understanding'. And I suspect that faith's at its strongest at the point when you hang on to nothing so to speak. I haven't been that far myself, but I was listening to a cassette the other day, and the priest who was talking was quoting St Thérèse of Lisieux, saying that in the last year of her life that was literally what she felt – that there was no God. And there's a fine balance between what you feel and whatever it is that makes you hang on: it's certainly not an intellectual conviction that keeps you going. Faith is an intangible something that makes you continue along this path through the religious life – even when the path is seemingly non-existent.

There's a quotation I've been trying to remember while I've been talking to you this week, and I think it's from James Michener's *The Source*. There was a bit in there where he said: 'Man is born with his hands clenched and he dies with his hands open.' And to me this is what the religious life is all about. It's about a letting go on all sorts of levels, and the vows we take are the expression of that, a starting point.

The *end* in living a life of poverty like this is to make a person free to relate to God, and to others. The end in itself is not destitution. It's a having – I was going to say 'without possessing' – but it's a having without *being* possessed. None of us is totally free, of course, however much we might like to think we were. But there are all the non-material sacrifices of this life too, like being thought well of, or being remembered or noticed or important. I see the striving to free myself from *these* things as part of poverty. But when I started, poverty was simply a material thing, a paring things down to the nitty-gritty. And then I realised how proud I was of the fact that I had less than most people – which rather spoilt the picture and made me realise that somewhere I was missing the point!

Poverty for us as Poor Clares is actually referred to as 'the *privilege* of poverty,' because Clare really had to fight for us to have no material possessions. In her day every monastery had to have endowments, and she only got permission on her deathbed not to have them. She said: 'We don't want material security. We want security in God.' And that's something we still try to cling to. Of course, it's very difficult to work out *how* you do this on a material level. The print room has recently got a computer because it saves a lot of work, but the ultimate reason for getting it was that it actually produced better work for the people we're working for. We try to use this sort of criterion for the work we do, but in other areas we try not to have the best.

On a personal level we all have different needs, and if you saw different people's rooms you would see how different their needs are. I have a bed and a locker. The bed is something I made out of an old divan, it's got drawers underneath, so most of my clothing sort of fits in there. And a chair. In terms of possessions there's my rosary. I bought it when I was fifteen for three and six. I think that's all actually. Oh well, yes, my clothes are mine. I've also got a very well-stocked toolbox, and in a sense I would call my tools mine: if somebody borrowed something without asking they would suddenly become very much mine! Which is when I know how un-free I am! My watch? Well, actually my watch packed up, and Mother Abbess gave me this two and a half years ago, it's one that her father left her. It's mine in so far as I'm using it, but I'd never have a second one.

I mean if I walked out of the house, which is perhaps the easiest way of looking at what's mine, I would obviously take – I was just trying to think what I brought when I came here. I know people were surprised by how little I brought. Clothing, breviaries, a Jerusalem bible, and four years later I gave that to a young girl going out to Uganda where they didn't have anything as sophisticated. Yes, that's about it.

Some funny things have been a great wrench. I prepared some children for confirmation this year, which I have done for several years, and I always give them a little present of some sort. We used to have a repository and I've always been able to take things from there, but we've ceased to restock it. Well, I had a black wall-plaque of Our Lady, a head and shoulders, which a child had given me years before. It's very beautiful, and I thought well, I could give that to one of them, I don't really need it. And it was *weeks* that I sat thinking about it. And in the end I thought, 'Look, take it off the wall and put it in the cupboard and get used to the gap on the wall.' So I did that. But it was hard, and I was surprised at how hard it was.

To some extent we each have to find the level that suits us, whilst striving for the ideal as honestly as we can. Financially, we are supposed to support ourselves, though the amount of money we earn as a community would never support us. We all work hard, but if you live in a place this size, maintenance eats away most of the money. It costs so much just to heat. We do have heating, don't get me wrong – look, there are pipes there – but you're not the only one who thinks that our heating is non-existent.

In terms of security, we pay people's insurance stamp until they've taken their Final Vows, but not afterwards. We don't build up financial securities. Most people would say this is ridiculously improvident, but it works: we're never without. Certainly a lot of time we're the wrong side of the red line, but time and time again, just as we're scraping the bottom of the barrel, something happens. We don't go out questing as used to be done in the past because it's not encouraged either by the Church or the state, but somebody always leaves us a legacy or whatever. Last year, for example, we had to have a lot of repairs done, including having the steeple completely reshingled, and we were getting in quite a panic. Within the diocese there was a fund for contemplative communities that we had actually founded, and we'd never touched it, although apparently the diocese have been paying our heating bills out of it for a while – we didn't realise that. So we pitched into this very reluctantly, very shamefacedly almost, but when everything was completed and the last bill paid, the exact amount was given to us by someone. And the bursar said, 'You see. Trust God and He'll provide.'

So I think religious life will remain. I think God will always provide for it, if you like. Because it is a human institution, it is constantly evolving, but I think there will always be groups of people who choose to live in community as a way of creating a space in which to grow close to God. And I wouldn't be surprised to see this form of religious life remain as a basic structure, because the basic setting apart of a place for silence and prayer will always be necessary. Just from looking at history you can see how mankind has always had this need for God and prayer.

I was going to say 'prayer is just sitting and being' but I don't think that'll satisfy you. I think prayer is very much a relationship between two people, the second person being God – and if you ask me what God is I'll say 'I don't know'! God *is*. And like any relationship, it will grow slowly. Although you get some relationships which burst into being, most relationships have to be worked at, and it's no different with God. It has peak periods, and then there'll be the times when God's away and you're sitting there alone and wondering when on earth he'll be back – or *if* he'll be back.

I've come to an understanding of prayer, in fairly recent years I suppose, as total gift – as the love of another person is total gift. I can never demand it. I can never expect it to feel good all the time. I've been conscious that prayer can be a really sort of 'wow' experience, you know, when you come away and you think, 'Goodness, what happened?' and there's no way that you can ever *make* it happen. All you can say is, 'Here I am, Lord.' The more you learn to sit with your hands open, so to speak, in the assurance that He will come – and there can be months at a time when you do that – the more you can do that, the better.

But God *cares* about you, He really does. He *wants* you to be able to share your happiness and your sorrow with Him. He's waiting for us to say, 'I love you, I need you.' He wants us to be able to sit with Him and say, 'I'm cheesed off today. Everybody seems to be being rotten to me, and I know it's me being rotten to them and I don't know what to do about it.' He wants us to sit there and know that however grotty we feel He loves us just the same. But God never suggested He'd give us a soft option. He never said, 'It's all going to be nice and tidy and mapped out and you say please and I say yes.' What He did say was: 'All things will work together unto good' for those who love Him.

JOHN McGAHERN

THE WINE BREATH

If I were to die, I'd miss most the mornings and the evenings, he thought as he walked the narrow dirt-track by the lake in the late evening, and then wondered if his mind was failing, for how could anybody think anything so stupid: being a man he had no choice, he was doomed to die; and being dead he'd miss nothing, being nothing. It went against everything in his life as a priest.

The solid world, though, was everywhere around him. There was the lake, and road, the evening, and he was going to call on Gillespie. Gillespie was sawing. Gillespie was always sawing. The roaring rise-and-fall of the two-stroke stayed like a rent in the evening. When he got to the black gate there was Gillespie, his overalled bulk framed in the short avenue of alders, and he was sawing not alders but beech, four or five tractor-loads dumped in the front of the house. The priest put a hand to the black gate, bolted to the first of the alders, and was at once arrested by showery sunlight falling down the avenue. It lit up one boot holding the length of beech in place, it lit the arms moving the blade slowly up and down as it tore through the beech, white chips milling out on the chain.

Suddenly, as he was about to rattle the gate loudly to see if this would penetrate the sawing, he felt himself (bathed as in a dream) in an incredible sweetness of light. It was evening light on snow. The gate on which he had his hand vanished, the alders, Gillespie's formidable bulk, the roaring of the saw. He was in another day, the lost day of Michael Bruen's funeral nearly thirty years before. All was silent and still there. Slow feet crunched on the snow. Ahead, at the foot of the hill, the coffin rode slowly forward on shoulders, its brown varnish and metal trappings dull in the glittering snow, riding just below the long waste of snow eight or ten feet deep over the whole countryside. The long dark line of mourners following the coffin stretched away towards Oak-port Wood in the pathway cut through the snow. High on Killeelan Hill the graveyard evergreens rose out of the snow. The graveyard wall was covered, the narrow path cut up the side of the hill stopping at the little gate deep in the snow. The coffin climbed with painful slowness, as if it might never reach the gate, often pausing for the bearers to be changed; and someone started to pray, the prayer travelling down the whole mile-long line of mourners as they shuffled behind the coffin in the narrow tunnel cut in the snow.

It was the day in February 1947 that they buried Michael Bruen. Never before or since had he experienced the Mystery in such awesomeness. Now, as he stood at the gate, there was no awe or terror, only the coffin moving slowly towards the dark trees on the hill, the long line of the mourners, and everywhere the blinding white light, among the half-buried thorn bushes and beyond Killeelan, on the covered waste of Gloria Bog, on the sides of Slieve an Iarainn.

He did not know how long he had stood in that lost day, in that white light, probably for no more than a moment. He could not have stood the intensity for any longer. When he woke out of it the grey light of the alders had reasserted itself. His hand was still on the bar of the gate. Gillespie was still sawing, bent over the saw-horse, his boot on the length of beechwood, completely enclosed in the roaring rise-and-fall of the saw. The priest felt as vulnerable as if he had suddenly woken out of sleep, shaken and somewhat ashamed to have been caught asleep in the actual day and life, without any protection of walls.

He was about to rattle the gate again, feeling a washed-out parody of a child or old man on what was after all nothing more than a poor errand: to tell the Gillespies that a bed had at long last been made available in the Regional Hospital for the operation on Mrs Gillespie's piles, when his eyes were caught again by the quality of the light. It was one of those late October days, small white clouds drifting about the sun, and the watery light was shining down the alder rows to fall on the white chips of the beechwood strewn all about Gillespie, some inches deep. It was the same white light as the light on snow. As he watched, the light went out on the beech chips, and it was the grey day again around Gillespie's sawing. It had been as simple as that. The suggestion of snow had been enough to plunge him into the lost day of Michael Bruen's funeral. Everything in that remembered day was so pure and perfect that he felt purged of all tiredness, was, for a moment, eager to begin life again.

Making sure that Gillespie hadn't noticed him at the gate, he turned back. The bed wouldn't be ready for another week. The news could wait a day or more. Before leaving he stole a last look at the dull white ground about the saw-horse. The most difficult things always seem to lie closest to us, to lie around our feet.

Ever since his mother's death he found himself stumbling into these dead days. Once, crushed mint in the garden had given him back a day he'd spent with her at the sea in such reality that he had been frightened, as if he'd suddenly fallen through time; it was as if the world of the dead was as available to him as the world of the living. It was also humiliating for him to realise that she must have been the mainspring of his days. Now that the mainspring was broken, the hands were weakly falling here and failing there. Today there had been the sudden light on the bits of white beech. He'd not have noticed it if he hadn't been alone, if Gillespie had not been so absorbed in his sawing. Before, there must have been some such simple trigger that he'd been too ashamed or bewildered to notice.

Stealthily and quickly he went down the dirt-track by the lake till he got to the main road. To the left was the church in a rookery of old trees, and behind it the house where he lived. Safe on the wide main road he let his mind go back to the beech chips. They rested there around Gillespie's large bulk, and paler still was the line of mourners following the coffin through the snow, a picture you could believe or disbelieve but not be in. In idle exasperation he began to count the trees in the hedge along the road as he walked: ash, green oak, whitheorn, ash; the last leaves a vivid yellow on the wild cherry, empty October fields in dull wet light behind the hedges. This, then, was the actual day, the only day that mattered, the day from which our salvation had to be won or lost: it stood solidly and impenetrably there, denying the weak life of the person, with nothing of the eternal other than it would dully endure, while the day set alight in his mind by the light of the white beech, though it had been nothing more than a funeral he had attended during a dramatic snowfall when a boy, seemed bathed in the eternal, seemed everything we had been taught and told of the world of God.

Dissatisfied, and feeling as tired again as he'd been on his way to Gillespie's, he did not go through the church gate with its circle and cross, nor did he call to the sexton locking up under the bell rope. In order to be certain of being left alone he went by the circular path at the side. A high laurel hedge hid the path from the graveyard and church. There he made coffee without turning on the light. Always when about to give birth or die cattle sought out a clean place in some corner of the field.

Michael Bruen had been a big kindly agreeable man, what was called a lovely man. His hair was a coarse grey. He wore loose-fitting tweeds with red cattleman's boots. When young he had been a policeman in Dublin. It was said he had either won or inherited money, and had come home to where he'd come from to buy the big Crossna farm, to marry and grow rich.

He had a large family. Men were employed on the farm. The yard and its big outhouses with the red roofs rang with work: cans, machinery, raillery, the sliding of hooves, someone whistling. Within the house, away from the yard, was the enormous cave of a kitchen, the long table down its centre, the fireplace at its end, the plates and pots and presses along the walls, sides of bacon wrapped in gauze hanging from hooks in the ceiling, the whole room full of the excitement and bustle of women.

Often as a boy the priest had gone to Michael Bruen's on some errand for his father. Once the beast was housed or the load emptied Michael would take him into the kitchen. The huge fire of wood blazed all the brighter because of the frost.

'Give this man something.' Michael had led him. 'Something solid that'll warm the life back into him.'

'A cup of tea will do fine,' he had protested in the custom.

'Nonsense. Don't pay him the slightest attention. Empty bags can't stand.'

Eileen, the prettiest of Michael's daughters, laughed as she took down the pan. Her arms were white to the elbows with a fine dusting of flour.

'He'll remember this was a good place to come to when he has to start thinking about a wife.' Michael's words gave licence to general hilarity.

It was hard to concentrate on Michael's questions about his father, so delicious was the smell of frying. The mug of steaming tea was put by his side. The butter melted on the fresh bread on the plate. There were sausages, liver, bacon, a slice of black-pudding and sweetest grisceens.

'Now set to,' Michael laughed. 'We don't want any empty bags leaving Bruen's.'

Michael came with him to the gate when he left. 'Tell your father it's ages since we had a drink in the Royal. And that if he doesn't search me out in the Royal the next Fair Day I'll have to go over and bate the lugs off him.' As he shook his hand in the half-light of the yard lamp it was the last time he was to see him alive. Before the last flakes had stopped falling, when old people were searching back to 'the great snows when Count Plunkett was elected' to find another such fall, Michael Bruen had died, and his life was already another such watermark of memory.

The snow lay eight feet deep on the roads, and dead cattle and sheep were found in drifts of fifteen feet in the fields. All of the people who hadn't lost sheep or cattle were in extraordinary good humour, their own ills buried for a time as deep as their envy of any other's good fortune in the general difficulty of the snow. It took days to cut a way out to the main road, the snow having to be cut in blocks breast-high out of a face of frozen snow. A wild cheer went up as the men at last cut through to the gang digging in from the main road. Another cheer greeted the first van to come in, Doherty's bread van, and it had hardly died when the hearse came with the coffin for Michael Bruen. That night they cut the path up the side of Killeelan Hill and found the family headstone beside the big yew just inside the gate and opened the grave. They hadn't finished digging when the first funeral bell came clearly over the snow the next day to tell them that the coffin had started on its way.

The priest hadn't thought of the day for years or of Michael Bruen till he had stumbled into it without warning by way of the sudden light on the beech chips. It did not augur well. There were days, especially of late, when he seemed to be lost in dead days, to see time present as a flimsy accumulating tissue over all the time that was lost. Sometimes he saw himself as an old man children were helping down to the shore, restraining the tension of their need to laugh as they pointed out a rock in the path he seemed about to stumble over, and then they had to lift their eyes and smile apologetically to the passersby while he stood staring out to sea, having forgotten all abut the rock in his path. 'It's this way we're going.' He felt the imaginary tug on his sleeve, and he was drawn again into the tortuous existence of the everyday, away from the eternal of the sea or the lost light on frozen snow across Killeelan Hill.

Never before though had he noticed anything like the beech chips. There was the joy of holding what had eluded him so long, in its amazing simplicity: but mastered knowledge was no longer knowledge unless it opened, became part of a greater knowledge, and what did the beech chips do but turn back to his own death?

Like the sudden snowfall and Michael Bruen's burial his life had been like any other, except to himself, and then only in odd visions of it, as a lost life. When it had been agreeable and equitable he had no vision of it at all.

The country childhood. His mother and father. The arrival at the shocking knowledge of birth and death. His attraction to the priesthood as a way of vanquishing death and avoiding birth. O hurry it, he thought. There is not much to a life. Many have it. There is not enough room. His father and mother were old when they married; he was 'the fruit of old things', he heard derisively. His mother had been a seamstress. He could still see the needle flashing in her strong hands, that single needle-flash composed of thousands of hours.

'His mother had the vocation for him.' Perhaps she had, perhaps all the mothers of the country had, it had so passed into the speech of the country, in all the forms of both beatification and derision; but it was out of fear of death he became a priest, which became in time the fear of life. Wasn't it natural to turn back to the mother in this fear? She was older than fear, having given him his life, and who would give a life if they knew its end? There was, then, his father's death, his acceptance of it, as he had accepted all poor fortune all his life long as his due, refusing to credit the good.

And afterwards his mother sold the land to 'Horse' McLaughlin and came to live with him and was happy. She attended all the Masses and Devotions, took messages, and she sewed, though she had no longer any need, linen for the altar, soutanes and surplices, his shirts and all her own clothes. Sometimes her concern for him irritated him to exasperation but he hardly ever let it show. He was busy with the many duties of a priest. The fences on the past and future were secure. He must have been what is called happy, and there was a whole part of his life that, without his knowing, had come to turn to her for its own expression.

He discovered it when she began her death. He came home one summer evening to find all the lights on in the house. She was in the living-room, in the usual chair. The table was piled high with dresses. Round the chair was a pile of rags. She did not look up when he entered, her still strong hands tearing apart a herring-bone skirt she had made only the year before.

'What on earth are you doing, Mother?' He caught her by the hands when she didn't answer.

'It's time you were up for Mass,' she said.

'What are you doing with your dresses?'

'What dresses?'

'All the dresses you've just been tearing up.'

'I don't know anything about dresses,' and then he saw there was something wrong. She made no resistance when he led her up the stairs.

For some days she seemed absent and confused but, though he

watched her carefully, she was otherwise very little different from her old self, and she did not appear ill. Then he came home one evening to find her standing like a child in the middle of the room, surrounded by an enormous pile of rags. She had taken up from where she'd been interrupted at the herring-bone skirt and torn up every dress or article of clothing she had ever made. After his initial shock he sent for the doctor.

'I'm afraid it's just the onset of senility,' the doctor said.

'It's irreversible?'

The doctor nodded, 'It very seldom takes such a violent form, but that's what it is. She'll have to be looked after.' With a sadness that part of his life was over, he took her to the Home and saw her settled there.

She recognised him when he visited her there the first year, but without excitement, as if he was already far away; and then the day came when he had to admit that she no longer knew who he was, had became like a dog kennelled out too long. He was with her when she died. She'd turned her face towards him. There came a light of recognition in the eyes like a last glow of a match before it goes out, and then she died.

There was nothing left but his own life. There had been nothing but that all along, but it had been obscured, comfortably obscured.

He turned on the radio.

A man had lost both legs in an explosion. There was violence on the night-shift at Ford's. The pound had steadied towards the close but was still down on the day.

Letting his fingers linger on the knob he turned it off. The disembodied voice on the air was not unlike the lost day he'd stumbled into through the light on the beech chips, except it had nothing of its radiance – the funeral during the years he carried it around with him lost the sheltered burden of the everyday, had become light as the air in all the clarity of light. It was all timeless, and seemed at least a promise of the eternal.

He went to draw the curtain. She had made the red curtain too with its pale lining but hadn't torn it. How often must she have watched the moonlight on the still headstones beyond the laurel as it lay evenly on them this night. She had been afraid of ghosts: old priests who had lived in this house, who through whiskey or some other ill had neglected to say some Mass for the dead and because of the neglect the soul for whom the Mass should have been offered was forced to linger beyond its time in Purgatory, and the priest guilty of the omission could himself not be released until the living priest had said the Mass, and was forced to come at midnight to the house in all his bondage until the Mass was said.

'They must have been all good priests, Mother. Good steady old fellows like myself. They never come back,' he used to assure her. He remembered his own idle words as he drew the curtain, lingering as much over the drawing of the curtain as he had lingered over the turning off of the radio. He would be glad of a ghost tonight, be glad of any visitation from beyond the walls of sense.

He took up the battered and friendly missal, which had been with him all his adult life, to read the office of the day. On bad days he kept it till late, the familiar words that changed with the changing year, that he had grown to love, and were as well his daily duty. It must be surely the greatest grace of life, the greatest freedom, to have to do what we love because it is also our duty. He wasn't able to read on this evening among the old familiar words for long. An annoyance came between him and the page, the Mass he had to repeat every day, the Mass in English. He wasn't sure whether he hated it or the guitar-playing priests more. It was humiliating to think that these had never been such a scourge when his mother had been alive. Was his life the calm vessel it had seemed, dully setting out and returning from the fishing grounds? Or had he been always what he seemed now? 'Oh yes. There you go again,' he heard the familiar voice in the empty room. 'Complaining about the Mass in the vernacular. When you prefer the common names of flowers to their proper names,' and the sharp, energetic, almost brutal laugh. It was Peter Joyce, he was not dead. Peter Joyce had risen to become a bishop at the other end of the country, an old friend he no longer saw.

'But they are more beautiful. Dog rose, wild woodbine, buttercup, daisy . . . '

He heard his own protest. It was in a hotel that they used to go to every summer on the Atlantic, a small hotel where you could read after dinner without fear of a rising roar from the bar beginning to outrival the Atlantic by ten o'clock.

'And, no doubt, the little rose of Scotland, sharp and sweet and breaks the heart,' he heard his friend quote maliciously. 'And it's not the point. The reason the names of flowers must be in Latin is that when flower lovers meet they know what they are talking about, no matter whether they're French or Greeks or Arabs. They have a universal language.'

'I prefer the humble names, no matter what you say.'

'Of course you do. And it's parochial sentimentalists like yourself who prefer the *smooth sowthistle* to *Sonchus oleraceus* that's the whole cause of your late lamented Mass in Latin disappearing. I have no sympathy with you. You people tire me.'

The memory of that truculent argument dispelled his annoyance, as its simple logic had once taken his breath away, but he was curiously tired after the vividness of the recall. It was only by a sheer act of will, sometimes having to count the words, that he was able to finish his office. 'I know one thing, Peter Joyce. I know that I know nothing,' he murmured when he finished. But when he looked at the room about him he could hardly believe it was so empty and dead and dry, the empty chair where she should be sewing, the oaken table with the scattered books, the clock on the mantel. Wildly and aridly he wanted to curse, but his desire to curse was as unfair as life. He had not wanted it.

Then, quietly, he saw that he had a ghost all right, one that he had been walking around with for a long time, a ghost he had not wanted to recognise – his own death. He might as well get to know him well. It would never leave now and had no mortal shape. Absence does not cast a shadow.

All that was there was the white light of the lamp on the open book, on the white marble; the brief sun of God on beechwood, and the sudden light of that glistening snow, and the timeless mourners moving towards the yews on Killeelan Hill almost thirty years ago. It was as good a day as any, if there ever was a good day to go.

Somewhere, outside this room that was an end, he knew that a young man, not unlike he had once been, stood on a granite step and listened to the doorbell ring, smiled as he heard a woman's footsteps come down the hallway, ran his fingers through his hair, and turned the bottle of white wine he held in his hands completely around as he prepared to enter a pleasant and uncomplicated evening, feeling himself immersed in time without end.

ANONYMOUS

COLUMCILLE THE SCRIBE

My hand is weary with writing,
My sharp quill is not steady,
My slender-beaked pen juts forth
A black draught of shining dark-blue ink.

A stream of the wisdom of blessed God
Springs from my fair-brown shapely hand:
On the page it squirts its draught
Of ink of the green-skinned holly.

My little dripping pen travels
Across the plain of shining books,
Without ceasing for the wealth of the great –
Whence my hand is weary with writing.

TRANSLATION: KUNO MEYER

LADY GREGORY

LAMENT FOR COLUMCILLE

This now is the poem of praise and of lamentation that was made for Columcille, Speckled Salmon of the Boinne, High Saint of the Gael, by Forgaill that was afterwards called Blind Forgaill, Chief Poet of Ireland:

'It is not a little story this is; it is not a story about a fool it is; it is not one district that is keening but every district, with a great sound that is not to be borne, hearing the story of Columcille, without life, without a church.

'It is not the trouble of one house, or the grief of one harpstring; all the plains are heavy, hearing the word that is a wound.

'What way will a simple man tell of him? Even Nera from the Sidhe could not do it; he is not made much of now; our learned one is not the light of our life now he is hidden away from us.

'He that used to keep us living is dead; he that was our rightful head has died from us; he has died from us, that was God's messenger.

'The knowledgeable man that used to put fear from us is not here; the teller of words does not return to us; the teacher is gone from us that taught silence to the people.

'The whole world was his; it is a harp without its strings; it is a church without its abbot.

'Colum rose very high the time God's companies rose to meet him; it is bright the angels were, attending on him.

'It is short his life was, it is little used to satisfy him; when the wind blew the sheet against him on the sand, the shape of his ribs could be seen through it.

'He was the head of every gathering; he was a dun of the book of the law; he put a flame in the district of the north, he lightened the district of the west; the east was his along with it; he did not open his heart to every company. Good his death; he went with God's angels that came to meet him.

'He has reached to Axal of his help and to the troops of the archangels; he has reached to a place where night is not seen; he has reached to a plain where music has not to be born; where no one listens to oppression. The King of priests has done away with his troubles.

'He knew the way he was going; he gave kindness for hatred; he learned psalms; he broke the battle against hunger.

'He knew seasons and storms; he read the secrets of the great wisdom; he knew the course of the moon; he took notice of its race with the branching sun. He was skilful in the course of the sea; to tell every high thing we have heard from Colum, would be to count the stars of heaven.

'A healer of the heart of the wise; a full satisfier of guests; our crowned one who spoke with Axal; a shelter to the naked; a comforter to the poor; he was eager, he was noble, it is high his death was. We hope great honour will be given to him on the head of these deeds.'

And when Forgaill had made that lament he said: 'It is a great shaping and a great finish I have given to these words, and I cannot make a praise beyond this, for my eyes have been taken from me.'

It was Aedh King of Ireland gave seven cumhals for his name to be given in the praising of Columcille; and Aedh laid it down to Forgaill that this song should be above every other song. But it was after death the reward and the praise were given to blind Forgaill; for it was Heaven that was given to him, as the price of the praising of the King.

PETER HEBBLETHWAITE

INTRODUCING ANGELO RONCALLI

I picture you, Pope John, in your vast bedroom on the top floor of the Apostolic Palace, not long before your eightieth birthday on November 25, 1961. Don't ask how I got in here. Let's just say your secretary, Don Loris Capovilla, fixed it (*Letture*, pp. 138-40, where John's room is described). He also tells me that your eyes are 'autumn-brown'.

You are standing at your window, overlooking St Peter's Square. Mgr Loris claims you never made that remark about 'opening the windows of the Vatican' that every journalist in the world has felt obliged to repeat. You didn't like draughts. Still, it was spiritually true, which is why they will go on saying it.

There goes the clock, chiming the hours with the Lourdes hymn – *Ave, ave Maria*, part of the furniture left behind by Pius XII. Your light goes on at four a.m., sometimes three. You said to Cardinal Antonio Bacci: 'I always get up at four in the morning; it's my time'. 'That's too early', he said timidly, 'even your holiness needs sleep'. And you replied: 'Yes, yes, sleep. But I also need to work . . . Anyway, one prays so well at first light, when everything is silent' (Bacci, p.93). In your eightieth year you don't need so much sleep. But you like a nap in the afternoon, always in an armchair, never in bed.

You keep your diaries and personal notes in this drawer over here, carefully catalogued. You started keeping a diary in 1895 as a record of graces received and to check if you were keeping your resolutions. Leo XIII was Pope then and much older then you are now. He was still Pope when you arrived in Rome, a raw provincial from Bergamo, in 1901.

Only the other day you dug out your retreat notes for that year, and underlined the passage which said that you had been 'led to Rome by the hand of Christ so that I may live under the protection of his Vicar, alongside the fountain of Catholic truth and the tomb of his apostles, where the very soil is stained with the blood of his martyrs, and the air is alive with the odour of sancity of his confessors' (*Journal*, p.95). So you needed your intercessors in the Communion of Saints then.

There's not much of the 'odour of sanctity' in Rome today as the cars cross and criss-cross out there in . . . Italy. Padre Pio, the famous Franciscan stigmatic, is said to emit 'the odour of roses'. You've never met him. You've nothing against him. But you prefer more ordinary and workaday virtues.

Mgr Loris tells me you have given him permission to publish your diaries after your death, because you believe they will help people. They will, no doubt, but it's a terrible risk, exposing yourself to the derision of the sophisticated, revealing your vulnerability, your naïveté. Some will fail to see that it is a record of growth in which the end crowns and explains the beginning. You want it to be knows as the *Journal of a Soul* on the model of St Theresa of Lisieux's *Story of a Soul*. I hope people will realise it is the *journey* of a soul, and that it is only a tiny selection from what you called 'sixty years spent with pen in hand'.

You never throw anything away, do you? You have your Mass intentions for every day of your life, and all the dog-eared passports and visas you ever collected. Is this the peasant in you, squirrel-like hanging on to everything 'in case it might come in handy some day'. Or is it rather your historian's instinct for the *document*, however apparently insignificant? It's the latter, obviously. You said that every diocese should keep its archives in a professional way.

Then there are all these statues which make your room look like a shop for religious bric-à-brac, if you'll forgive me. But they all have a meaning for you. Opposite the crucifix is St Mark, patron of Venice and *interpres Petri* (some translate this as Peter's secretary or amanuensis). Mark is flanked by the two Johns, the Baptist and the Evangelist. It was to honour them, and your father, that when for the first time in your life you could give yourself a name, you chose John. At least that was what you said. I suspect there were other motives.

Madonnas abound, icons picked up in Turkey and Greece, mediaeval paintings from France. There's your favourite Madonna of Covadonga. 'Through Mary to Jesus': how many times have you preached on that theme? You had it inscribed above the door of your chapel in Istanbul.

We've still not finished with statuary. Sts Peters and Paul: obvious why they are here, the pastor and the missionary. St Joseph: that is your middle name, and very soon you are going to surprise the Council by including his name in the canon of the Mass. St Charles Borromeo: your whole life was bound up with him: he was archbishop of Milan, he visited your diocese of Bergamo, you were ordained in his church on the Corso here in Rome where his heart is still kept, and your five volume edition of his episcopal visitations – over there on the shelf, proudly displayed, was the main literary work of your life. Unless, of course, you have something else up your sleeve, like a letter about peace to the whole world.

Here is St Francis de Sales, whose quality of gentle self-acceptance and unforced naturalness you always liked. Leigh Hunt, an English writer you won't have read called him 'the gentleman saint'. One of your problems in France was that you imagined all Frenchmen were going to be like St Francis de Sales. Now St Gregory Barbarigo is something of a poser. You knew all about him but I had to look him up. He started adult life as a Venetian diplomat, then became bishop of Bergamo, and emulated Charles Borromeo in implementing the Council of Trent. He was beatified in 1761. He then had to wait until 1960, last year, for you to canonise him. Yet another Italian saint, complained the foreign leader writers, but for you he was an old and familiar friend.

Then, of course, the obligatory busts of your immediate predecessors. Pius X and Pius XI both died in this very room. Benedict XV died next door. Pius XII died at Castelgandolfo. So much for statues.

The photographs are less daunting and more intimate. Your parents: Giovanni Battista Roncalli and Marianna Mazzola; the three deceased sisters, Teresa, Ancilla, and Maria, to whom you were so close; your three surviving brothers, Zaverio, Alfredo and Giuseppe who came to Rome for your coronation and fidgeted with their Sunday hats, solid peasants astonished to find themselves brothers of a pope. There's Giovanni, who died on September 18, 1956.

Now some clerics you'll have to explain for the uninitiated. Don Francesco Rubuzzini was the parish priest of Sotto il Monte. He baptised you the day you were born, taught you better than most of your teachers, and left you his copy of *The Imitation of Christ*.

To be more accurate, you just took it as a memento. Canon Giovanni Morlani who helped pay for your studies. Mgr Vincenzo Bugarini, rector of the Roman seminary, who died in your flat in 1922. Fr Francesco Pitocchi C.SS.R., invalid and spiritual director at the seminary. Then a group photograph of your class looking earnest and puddingy. The layman with long flowing beard is count Giovanni Grosoli, advocate of 'Catholic social doctrine', and owner at the start of the century of a newspaper chain.

But pride of place goes to Giacomo Radini Tedeschi, *your* bishop, whose secretary and biographer you were. You still describe him, with capital letters as '*il Mio Vescovo*'.

This lot of photographs show people you met in the East, beginning with the tragic King Boris and his Italian queen, Giovanna. These are all the bishops you ordained in Istanbul with their amazing variety of headgear. Here are pictures of the French bishops on your arrival as Nuncio in 1945 and on your departure in 1953: this would remind you how many had survived de Gaulle's 'purge'. Finally, two paintings: the cemetery at Sotto il Monte where most of your family is buried, but you will not be; and Cardinal Andrea Carlo Ferrari, archbishop of Milan, who died in 1921. A thesis has just rehabilitated him. He was your spiritual guide and friend.

So much of Pope John was gathered in what Capovilla calls his 'gallery'. His love for the saints of the gospel, and the saints of the Counter-Reformation. His loyalty to his modest family. His fidelity to the past and Bergamo. The sheer length of his life and diversity of his experience – he had lived for long periods in five different countries. His neglect of his own achievements – none of the photographs are of himself – and his attentiveness to others. His need for 'models' of the priestly and episcopal ministry. His sense of continuity in the office he now held.

But this collection was in the room of the man who happened to be pope. Anywhere else one might have been tempted to regard it as the dusty débris of a lifetime or the self-indulgence of a very old man who could not let go of the past. But he had already called an Ecumenical Council that would launch the Church on an adventure of hope. Far from being buried in the past, the old man had a keen eye for the contemporary world. He was always looking to the future, right up to the end. He was open to the Holy Spirit, whom he believed to be at work, burrowing away in the modern world. That was why he could surprise people.

His 'gallery' was like the iconostasis of an Orthodox church: the bond between earth and heaven in the communion of saints. People were always more important to him than ideas – or rather, he saw ideas as embodied in people: he was less interested in the decrees of the Council of Trent than in St Charles Borromeo who lived them as a reforming bishop. So here he was in the room where he will die, surrounded by saints, relatives, friends, and spiritual guides who were all involved in the onward rolling story of salvation.

Dates, anniversaries, birthdays were important to him. John entered salvation history in 1881. Also born in that year were four boys whose lives where to intersect with his own: Pierre Teilhard de Chardin, Jesuit, paleontologist, mystic; Ernesto Buonaiuti, his fellow-seminarian who was driven out of the Church as a 'Modernist'; Alcide De Gasperi, who spent the Second World War in the Vatican Library and emerged to lead the Christian Democrats; and Augustine Bea, another Jesuit, who became the founder-president of the Secretariat for Christian Unity. Angelo Giuseppe Roncalli came last in this vintage year. He was born on November 25.

A WAY OF LIFE

SAINT THÉRÈSE OF LISIEUX

THE LITTLE WAY

We must do everything we are obliged to do: give without reckoning, practice virtue whenever opportunity offers, constantly overcome ourselves, prove our love by all the little acts of tenderness and consideration we can muster. In a word, we must produce all the good works that lie within our strength – out of love for God. But it is in truth indispensable to place our whole trust in Him Who alone sanctifies our works and Who can sanctify us without works for He can even raise children to Abraham out of stones. Yes, it is needful, when we have done everything that we believe we have to do, to confess ourselves unprofitable servants, at the same time hoping that God out of grace will give us everything we need. This is the little way of childhood.

GUIGO THE CARTHUSIAN

LETTER

To the Reverend N., Guigo, least of those servants of the Cross who are in the Charterhouse: to live and to die for Christ. One man will think another happy. I esteem him happy above all who does not strive to be lifted up with great honours in a palace, but who elects, humble, to live like a poor countryman in a hermitage, who with thoughtful application loves to meditate in peace, who seeks to sit by himself in silence. For to shine with honours, to be lifted up with dignities, is to my judgement a way of little peace, subject to perils, burdened with cares, treacherous to many, and to none secure. Happy in the beginning, perplexed in its development, wretched in its end. Flattering to the unworthy, disgraceful to the good, generally deceptive to both. While it makes many wretched, it satisfies none, makes no one happy. But the poor and lonely life, hard in its beginning, easy in its progress, becomes, in its end, heavenly. It is constant in adversity, trusty in hours of doubt, modest in those of good fortune. Sober fare, simple garments, laconic speech, chaste manners. The highest ambition, because without ambition. Often wounded with sorrow at the thought of past wrong done, it avoids present, is wary of future evil. Resting on the hope of mercy, without trust in its own merit, it thirsts after heaven, is sick of earth, earnestly strives for right conduct, which it retains in constancy and holds for ever. It fasts with determined constancy in love of the Cross yet consents to eat for the body's need. In both it observes the greatest moderation, for when it dines it restrains greed and when it fasts, vanity. It is devoted to reading, but mostly in the scripture canon and in holy books, where it is more intent upon the inner marrow of meaning than on the spume of words. But you may praise or wonder more at this: that this life is continually idle yet never lazy. For it finds many things indeed to do, so that time is often lacking to it than this or that occupation. It more often laments that its time has slipped away than that its business is tedious. What else? A happy subject, to advise leisure, but such an exhortation seeks a mind that is its own master, concerned with its own business, disdaining to be caught up in the affairs of others, or of society. Who so fights as a soldier of Christ in peace as to refuse double service as a soldier of God and a hireling of the world. Who knows for sure it cannot here be glad with this world and then, in the next, reign with God. Small matters are these, and their like, if you recall what drink He took at the gibbet, who calls you to kingship. Like it or not, you must follow the example of Christ poor if you would have fellowship with Christ in His riches. If we suffer with Him, says the Apostle, we will reign with Him. If we die with Him, then we shall live together with Him. The Mediator Himself replied to the two disciples who asked Him if one of them might sit at His right hand and the other at His left: Can you drink the chalice which I am about to drink? Here He made clear that it is by cups of earthly bitterness that we come to the banquet of the Patriarchs and to the nectar of heavenly celebrations. Since friendship strengthens confidence I charge, advise and beg you, my best beloved in Christ, dear to me since the day I knew you, that as you are farseeing, careful, learned and most acute, take care to save the little bit of life that remains still unconsumed, snatch it from the world, light under it the fire of love to burn it up as an evening sacrifice to God, and delay not, but be like Christ both priest and victim, in an odour of sweetness to God and to men. Now that you may fully understand the drift of all my argument, I appeal to your wise judgement in few words with what is at once the counsel and desire of my soul. Undertake our observance as a man of great heart and noble deeds, for the sake of your eternal salvation. Become a recruit of Christ and stand guard in the camp of the heavenly army, watchful with your sword on your thigh against the terrors of the night. Here then I advise you to a thing that is good to undertake, easy to carry out and happy in its consummation. Let prayers be said, I beg you, that in carrying out so worthy a business you may exert yourself in proportion to the grace that will smile on you in God's favour. As to where or when you must do this thing, I leave it to the choice of your own prudence. But to delay, or to hesitate will not, as I believe, serve your turn. I will proceed no further with this, for fear that rough and uncouth lines might offend you, a man of palaces and courts. An end and a measure then, to this letter but never an end to my affection or love for you.

TRANSLATION: THOMAS MERTON

WILLIAM BLAKE

A DIVINE IMAGE

Cruelty has a Human Heart,
And Jealousy a Human face;
Terror the Human Form Divine,
And Secrecy the Human Dress.

The Human Dress is forged Iron,
The Human Form a fiery Forge,
The Human face a Furnace seal'd,
The Human Heart its hungry Gorge.

GOD

THOMAS MERTON

PRAYER

My Lord God, I have no idea where I am going. I do not see the road ahead of me. I cannot know for certain where it will end. Nor do I really know myself, and the fact that I think I am following your will does not mean that I am actually doing so. But I believe that the desire to please you does in fact please you. And I hope I have that desire in all that I am doing. I hope that I will never do anything apart from that desire. And I know that if I do this you will lead me by the right road, though I may know nothing about it. Therefore I will trust you always though I may seem to be lost and in the shadow of death. I will not fear, for you are ever with me, and you will never leave me to face my perils alone.

SAINT PATRICK

THE DEER'S CRY

I arise to-day
Through a mighty strength, the invocation of the Trinity,
Through belief in the threeness,
Through confession of the oneness
Of the Creator of Creation.

I arise to-day
Through the strength of Christ's birth with His baptism,
Through the strength of His crucifixion with His burial,
Through the strength of His resurrection with His ascension,

MEISTER ECKHART

THE IMPORTANCE OF THE TRIVIAL

Meister Eckhart's good friends bade him: 'Since you are going to leave us, give us one last word.'

'I will give you,' he replied, 'a rule which is the stronghold of all I have ever said, in which are lodged all the truths to be discussed or put into practice.'

It often happens that what seems trivial to us is more important to God than what we think important. Therefore, we ought to take everything God puts on us evenly, not comparing and wondering which is more important, or higher, or best. We ought simply to follow where God leads, this is, to do what we are most inclined to do, to go where we are repeatedly admonished to go – to where we feel most drawn. If we do that, God gives us his greatest in our least and never fails.

Now, some people despise the little things of life. It is their mistake, for they thus prevent themselves from getting God's greatness out of these little things. God is every way, evenly in all ways, to him who has the eyes to see. But sometimes it is hard to know whether one's inclinations come from God or not, but that can be decided this way: If you find yourself always possessed of a knowledge or intimation of God's will, which you obey before everything else, because you feel urged to obey it and the urge is frequent, then you may know that it is from God.

Some people want to recognise God only in some pleasant enlightenment – and then they get pleasure and enlightenment but not God. Somewhere it is written that God shines in the darkness where every now and then we get a glimpse of him. More often, God is where his light is least apparent. Therefore we ought to expect God in all manners and all things evenly.

Someone may now say: I should be glad to look for God evenly in all shapes and things, but my mind does not always work the same way – and then, not as well with this as with that. To which I reply: That is too bad! All paths lead to God and he is on them all evenly, to him who knows. I am well aware that a person may get more out of one technique than another but it is not best so. God responds to all techniques evenly to a knowing man. Such and such may be the way, but it is not God.

But even if God is in all ways and all things evenly, do I not still need a special way to get to him? Let us see. Whatever the way that leads you most frequently to awareness of God, follow that way; and if another way appears, different from the first, and you quit the first and take the second, and the second works, it is all right. It would be nobler and better, however, to achieve rest and security through evenness, by which one might take God and enjoy him in any manner, in any thing, and not have to delay and hunt around for your special way: *that has been my joy!* To this end all kinds of activities may contribute and any work may be a help; but if it does not, let it go!

HILDEGARD OF BINGEN

A BRILLIANT FIRE

In the year 1142, when I was forty-two years and seven months old, it happened that a great light of brilliant fire came from the open heavens and overwhelmed all my mind, my heart, and my breast, not so much like a flickering flame, but rather like glowing heat, as the sun warms other things on which it sheds its rays. And suddenly I had the power of explaining scripture, not by a word-for-word interpretation, nor a division of syllables, or cases or tenses. From the time I was a little girl about five years old, I was conscious of a mysterious hidden power and experienced wonderful visions within myself, but told them to none except for a few religious with whom I lived. And during that time until the grace of God wished them to be made known, I hid them under strict silence. These visions which I saw were not in sleep nor in dreams, nor in my imagination nor by bodily eyes or outward ears nor in a hidden place; but in watching, aware with the pure eyes of the mind and inner ear of the heart. But I received them while wide awake, according to the will of God. How this happened it is difficult for mortal men to understand.

EVELYN UNDERHILL

THE SPIRITUAL LIFE

I come now to the many people who, greatly desiring the life of communion with God, find no opportunity for attention to Him in an existence that often lacks privacy, and is conditioned by ceaseless household duties, exacting professional responsibilities or long hours of work. The great spiritual teachers, who are not nearly so aloof from normal life as those who do not read them suppose, have often dealt with this situation, which is not new, though it seems to press with peculiar weight upon ourselves. They all give the same answer: that what is asked of us is not necessarily a great deal of time devoted to what we regard as spiritual things, but the constant offering of our wills to God, so that the practical duties that fill most of our days can become part of His order and be given spiritual worth. So Père Grou, whose writings are among the best and most practical guides to the spiritual life that we possess, says, 'We are always praying, when we are doing our duty and turning it into work for God.' He adds that among the things we should regard as spiritual in this sense are our household or professional work, our social duties, friendly visits, kind actions and small courtesies, and also necessary recreation of body and of mind, so long as we link all these by intention with God and the great movement of His will.

So those who wonder where they are to begin, might begin here; by trying to give spiritual quality to every detail of their everyday lives, whether those lives are filled with a constant succession of home duties, or form part of the great systems of organised industry or public service, or are devoted to intellectual or artistic ends. The same lesson is taught by George Herbert's poem: –

Who sweeps a room as for Thy laws,
Makes that and the action fine –

Through the strength of His descent for the judgment of Doom.

I arise to-day
Through the strength of the love of Cherubim,
In obedience of angels,
In the service of archangels,
In hope of resurrection to meet with reward,
In prayers of patriarchs,
In predictions of prophets,
In preaching of apostles,
In faiths of confessors,
In innocence of holy virgins,
In deeds of righteous men.

I arise to-day
Through the strength of heaven:
Light of sun,
Radiance of moon,
Splendour of fire,
Speed of lightning,
Swiftness of wind,
Depth of sea,
Stability of earth,
Firmness of rock.

I arise to-day,
Through God's strength to pilot me:
God's might to uphold me,
God's wisdom to guide me,
God's eye to look before me,
God's ear to hear me,
God's word to speak for me,
God's hand to guard me,
God's way to lie before me,
God's shield to protect me,
God's host to save me
From snares of devils,
From temptations of vices,
From every one who shall wish me ill,
Afar and anear,
Alone and in a multitude.

I summon to-day all these powers between me and those evils,
Against every cruel merciless power that may oppose my body and
                            soul,
Against incantations of false prophets,
Against black laws of pagandom,
Against false laws of heretics,
Against craft of idolatry,
Against spells of women and smiths and wizards,
Against every knowledge that corrupts man's body and soul.

Christ to shield me to-day
Against poison, against burning,
Against drowning, against wounding,
So that there may come to me abundance of reward.
Christ with me, Christ before me, Christ behind me,
Christ in me, Christ beneath me, Christ above me,
Christ on my right, Christ on my left,
Christ when I lie down, Christ when I sit down,
Christ when I arise,
Christ in the heart of every man who thinks of me,
Christ in the mouth of every one who speaks of me,
Christ in every eye that sees me,
Christ in every ear that hears me.

I arise to-day
Through a mighty strength, the invocation of the Trinity,
Through belief in the threeness,
Through confession of the oneness
Of the Creator of Creation.

TRANSLATION: KUNO MEYER

JOHN DONNE

I

Wilt Thou forgive that sin where I begun,
    Which was my sin, though it were done before?
Wilt Thou forgive that sin, through which I run,
    And do run still, though still I do deplore?
When Thou hast done, Thou hast not done,
        For I have more.

II

Wilt Thou forgive that sin which I have won
    Others to sin, and made my sin their door?
Wilt Thou forgive that sin which I did shun
    A year or two, but wallowed in a score?
When Thou hast done, Thou hast not done,
        For I have more.

III

I have a sin of fear, that when I have spun
    My last thread, I shall perish on the shore;
But swear by Thyself, that at my death Thy Son
    Shall shine as he shines now, and heretofore;
And, having done that, Thou hast done:
        I fear no more.

SAINT CATHERINE OF SIENA

A STAIRCASE TO GOD

Ah, dear child, may God give you what my heart desires for you,
and may you love him as he deserves. Still, I could never endure,
dear child, that someone before me loved God as dearly as I. I believe
that many loved him as fondly and dearly, yet I could hardly bear
that someone would know him with such passion.

To enable the soul to attain this perfection, Christ has made his body into a staircase, with great steps. See, his feet are nailed fast to the cross; they constitute the first great step because, to begin with, the soul's desire has to be stripped of self-will, for as the feet carry the body, so desire carries the soul. Reflect that no soul will ever acquire virtue without climbing this first step. Once you have done that, you come to real, deep humility. Climb the next step without delay and you reach the open side of God's Son. Within, you will find the fathomless furnace of divine charity. Yes, on this second step of the open side, there is a little shop, full of fragrant spices. Therein you will find the God-Man; therein, too, the soul becomes so satiated and inebriated as to become oblivious of self for, like a man intoxicated with wine, it will have eyes only for the blood spilt with such burning love. With eager longing it presses on upwards and reaches the last step, the mouth, where it reposes in peace and quiet, savouring the peace of obedience. Like a man who falls asleep after drinking heavily and so is oblivious of both pain and pleasure, the bride of Christ, brimming over with love, sleeps in the peace of her bridegroom. Her own feelings are so deeply asleep that she remains unruffled when assailed by tribulations and rises above undue delight in worldly prosperity; for she stripped herself of all desire of that kind back on the first step. Here on the third she is conformed to Christ crucified and made one with him.

HENRY VAUGHAN

THE WORLD

I saw Eternity the other night
Like a great *Ring* of pure and endless light,
    All calm, as it was bright,
And round beneath it, Time in hours, days, years
        Driv'n by the spheres
Like a vast shadow mov'd, in which the world
    And all her train were hurl'd;
The doting lover in his quaintest strain
        Did there complain,

Near him his lute, his fancy, and his flights,
    Wit's sour delights,
With gloves and knots, the silly snares of pleasure;
    Yet his dear treasure
All scattered lay, while he his eyes did pore
    Upon a flower.

The darksome statesman, hung with weights and woe,
Like a thick midnight-fog moved there so slow
    He did not stay, nor go;
Condemning thoughts (like sad eclipses) scowl
    Upon his soul,
And clouds of crying witnesses without
    Pursued him with one shout.
Yet digged the mole, and lest his ways be found
    Worked underground,
Where he did clutch his prey, but one did see
    That policy;
Churches and altars fed him, perjuries
    Were gnats and flies,
It rained about him blood and tears, but he
    Drank them as free.

The fearful miser on a heap of rust
Sat pining all his life there, did scarce trust
    His own hands with the dust,
Yet would not place one piece above, but lives
    In fear of thieves.
Thousand there were as frantic as himself
    And hugged each one his pelf,
The downright Epicure placed heaven in sense
    And scorned pretence
While others, slipped into a wide excess,
    Said little less;
The weaker sort slight, trivial wares enslave
    Who think them brave,
And poor, despisèd Truth sat counting by
    Their victory.
Yet some, who all this while did weep and sing,
And sing, and weep, soared up into the *Ring*,
    But most would use no wing.

'O fools' (said I) 'thus to prefer dark night
     Before true light,
To live in grots, and caves, and hate the day
    Because it shows the way,
The way which from this dead and dark abode
     Leads up to God,
A way where you might tread the sun, and be
     More bright than he.'
But as I did their madness so discuss
     One whispered thus:
'This Ring the Bridegroom did for none provide
     But for his bride.'

KING DAVID (ATTRIB.)

PSALM 90

He who dwells in the shelter of the Most High
and abides in the shade of the Almighty
says to the Lord: 'My refuge,
my stronghold, my God in whom I trust!'

It is he who will free you from the snare
of the fowler who seeks to destroy you;
he will conceal you with his pinions
and under his wings you will find refuge.

You will not fear the terror of the night
nor the arrow that flies by day,
nor the plague that prowls in the darkness
nor the scourge that lays waste at noon.

A thousand may fall at your side,
ten thousand fall at you right,
you, it will never approach;
his faithfulness is buckler and shield.

Your eyes have only to look
to see how the wicked are repaid,
you who have said: 'Lord, my refuge!'
and have made the Most High your dwelling.

Upon you no evil shall fall,
no plague approach where you dwell.
For you has he commanded his angels,
to keep you in all your ways.

They shall bear you upon their hands
lest you strike your foot against a stone.
On the lion and the viper you will tread
and trample the young lion and the dragon.

His love he set on me, so I will rescue him;
protect him for he knows my name.
When he calls I shall answer: 'I am with you.'
I will save him in distress and give him glory.

With length of life I will content him;
I shall let him see my saving power.

SAINT JOHN OF THE CROSS

SONGS OF THE SOUL IN RAPTURE

*Songs of the soul in rapture at having arrived at the height of perfection,
which is union with God by the road of spiritual negation.*

Upon a gloomy night,
with all my cares to loving ardours flushed,
(O venture of delight!)
With nobody in sight
I went abroad when all my house was hushed.

In safety, in disguise,
In darkness up the secret stair I crept,

(O happy enterprise!)
Concealed from other eyes
When all my house at length in silence slept.

Upon that lucky night
In secrecy, inscrutable to sight,
I went without discerning
And with no other light
Except for that which in my heart was burning.

It lit and let me through
More certain than the light of noonday clear
To where One waited near
Whose presence well I knew,
There where no other presence might appear.

Oh night that was my guide!
Oh darkness dearer than the morning's pride,
Oh night that joined the lover
To the beloved bride
Transfiguring them each into the other.

Within my flowering breast
Which only for himself entire I save
He sank into his rest
And all my gifts I gave
Lulled by the airs with which the cedars wave.

Over the ramparts fanned
While the fresh wind was fluttering his tresses,
With his serenest hand
My neck he wounded, and
Suspended every sense with its caresses.

Lost to myself I stayed
My face upon my lover having laid
From all endeavour ceasing:
And all my cares releasing
Threw them amongst the lilies there to fade.

TRANSLATION: ROY CAMPBELL

PASSION AND RESURRECTION

WILLIAM BLAKE

HOLY THURSDAY

'Twas on a Holy Thursday, their innocent faces clean,
The children walking two & two, in red & blue & green,
Grey-headed beadles walk'd before, with wands as white as snow,
Till into the high dome of Paul's they like Thames' waters flow.

O what a multitude they seem'd, these flowers of London town!
Seated in companies they sit with radiance all their own.
The hum of multitudes was there, but multitudes of lambs,
Thousands of little boys & girls raising their innocent hands.

Now like a mighty wind they raise to heaven the voice of song,
Or like harmonious thunderings the seats of heaven among.
Beneath them sit the aged men, wise guardians of the poor;
Then cherish pity, lest you drive an angel from your door.

MARGARET HEBBLETHWAITE

MARY OF BETHANY

My thoughts and prayers now had a new element: how could I show,
both that I gave Jesus everything, and that I recognised that he had
exchanged his life for that of Lazarus? How could I show that I
believed he was the Messiah – and that I knew he was a Messiah
who was about to be murdered?

What is more, time was running out. Jesus could be arrested
any day.

I did not talk about this with Martha: she would not have understood. Martha knew he was the Messiah, all right. She had been brave enough to say so, while everyone else kept quite because they were too embarrassed about looking foolish. And we had often talked about the danger surrounding Jesus. We had even asked each other more than once if we would ever see him again. But right now Martha was so happy about Lazaraus being alive that she was discounting the threats to Jesus. She thought, as everyone else did, that because he had revealed his power as Messiah so dramatically he had shown that he too would escape death. How did I know he was really going to die? It was simple: Jesus had said so. He had several times told his closest friends – and we of course were among his very closest friends – that he was going to Jerusalem to fall into the hands of the chief priests, to be mocked and spat on and scourged, and to be put to death. I cannot think why no one believed it other than me. And yet I knew he could still be the Messiah, because he also said he would rise from the dead on the third day.

And now my gesture had to be one that showed: that I loved him and poured out my thanks to him with the gift of all I had; that I recognised he was about to die, as a result of what he had done for me; and that even through this death, he was the Messiah. It was quite an undertaking.

I went into Jerusalem, to the temple, and I prayed for guidance. Then I came out and I wandered round the streets, cocooned in my thoughts amid the hubbub of people. I walked down the street that had the most expensive shops in the whole country, and I gazed at their displays. There were fine silks and gold ornaments, but they were not quite right for the king who was on the side of the poor.

One shop had jars of ointment, for anointing the bodies of the dead. I stopped, and looked more closely. Here was something that could be a sign of faith in his death. There were various oils and unguents, beginning at one denarius for a small jar, and rising in price from there. The finest – and most expensive – ointment was spikenard. I had smelled it once, and knew there was nothing to match it. They were selling it in alabaster jars, and I looked at the different sizes – there was one at 30 denarii, one at 50, and one at 100. And then there was the most beautiful, big jar: the label said there was a pound's weight of ointment there, and it cost 300 denarii. Three hundred denarii! Why, it would take a labourer 300 days to earn enough to pay for that! You could say that alabaster jar of pure nard was worth nearly a year of my life.

My heart skipped a few beats and I walked quickly on. An

argument was raging inside me. One side said, 'Don't be a bloody fool, Mary. Don't lose your head. Don't be absurd.' The other side said, 'Only a year of your life? Not quite a year? What is that? Didn't you say you wanted to give Jesus all the years of your life?' The first side said, 'Look here, Mary, you know perfectly well that 300 denarii is your entire savings. You wouldn't have a penny left for your old age, or for giving to charity, or for emergencies.' The other side said, 'Remember how Jesus taught you not to store things up for the future, but to be as poor as a lily of the field.' The first side said, 'Buy a smaller jar, for heaven's sake, it's only supposed to be symbolic.' The other side said, 'How can you give Jesus second best, especially at such a moment, when he is about to die?'

I didn't breathe a word to Martha or Lazarus, though they sensed I was brooding and tried to cheer me up and chivvy me along. But I would not be drawn, and would not be bounced out of my preoccupation. I had a big decision to make.

By the next morning it was made. I dug up the box of my savings (it was buried for safety in a hidden place), went back to Jerusalem, and came back with the large and fragile jar. I was terrified I would drop it on the way home, especially since I was so embarrassed about it I was carrying it underneath my cloak. I hid it in my room, and went and helped Martha in the kitchen – much more cheerful now it was too late to change my mind.

What I now had to wait for was Jesus' next visit, hoping there would be a next visit. Supposing we never saw him again? His end must be very close. Please God may Jesus come before it is too late.

In those days of waiting – they were few days, but they passed slowly – I prepared myself for what I had committed myself to do. I prayed and I read the scriptures. And the more I read, the more awesome I found my task.

I discovered, to my amazement, that anointing could be a most sacred act, hedged around with warnings against sacrilege if anyone took it into their own hands to anoint the wrong person. God instructed Moses to take the finest spices and make of them a sacred anointing oil. Then Moses was told to anoint Aaron and his sons, so that by this act of consecration they would serve God as priests. The anointing oil was holy, and was not to be poured on any ordinary person, for the one on whose head the anointing oil was poured was exalted above his fellows. Anyone who did so or who tried to imitate this religious rite of anointing was to be cut off from the people.

By solemnly anointing Jesus for his forthcoming sacrifice, with the finest, purest, most fragrant oil, would I not be sharing in this religious act? What Moses did to Aaron, would I not be doing to Jesus? Would I not be anointing him, and ordaining him, and consecrating him, so that he might serve God as a priest? But was not my act an even more sacred act, for an even greater high priest, who would make an even more holy offering? Surely if the priests at Jerusalem had any inkling of what I was doing they would cast me out with terrible anger.

I read on, with growing alarm. I discovered that anointing was a sign not only of priesthood, but also of kingship. I read how God revealed to Samuel that he was to anoint Saul to be king of Israel, to save the people from their suffering. Samuel woke Saul at the break of dawn and brought him alone into the deserted streets. He took a vial of oil and poured it on his head, and kissed him. And then the Spirit of God entered Saul, so that he prophesised. So was I to pour the oil on Jesus' head? And to kiss him? And would he then be empowered by God's Spirit to carry out his mission as king of Israel, and to save the people from their suffering?

I read also how Samuel anointed David to be king, in the place of Saul. He took a horn of oil and anointed David in the presence of his brothers, and the Spirit of God came mightily upon David from that day forward. Was I to pay the role of Samuel? He had been unique in the history of our people, for he was a prophet who became judge over Israel – the highest political and spiritual authority in the land and a precursor of the monarch. Was I, a woman, to anoint someone greater than David? Was I to consecrate the Messiah, the anointed one of God?

I read still further. I read how the prophet Elijah was commissioned by God to anoint kings and to anoint Elisha as prophet in his place. So anointing had a threefold significance. I was to anoint Jesus as priest, king and prophet. And I was to follow in the footsteps of not only Moses and Samuel, but Elijah too. And then I remembered that our scribes taught us that Elijah must come again, before the great day of the Messiah.

I was humbled, frightened, and overwhelmed. But I could not back off now, for I had bought the alabaster jar for 300 denarii. All I could do was hope that Jesus never came again, so that I would never have the chance to anoint him. That way the decision would be taken out of my hands.

But Jesus did come. Six days before the Passover he came to

dinner with us. It was to be now or never. I knew he would never come again. Lazarus was there, surrounded by happy friends congratulating Jesus on this living, breathing evidence of his power. Martha served the meal and presided over the occasion, with dignity, gratitude and pride. I was the only person at table to be quiet and moody. Jesus was certainly not moody, though I did feel he had an air of sadness, as though he was carrying a burden.

I could not eat much, and I slipped out halfway through the meal. No one suspected: they would have thought I was going to the kitchen. Instead I went to my room and knelt on the floor. I prayed with desperation. Then I undid my hair and let it fall freely. I took out my precious vase, and carried it in front of me with slow solemnity into the dining room. I kept my eyes fixed rigidly on the vase: it was a luminous creamy white, with the lightest of grains, cool as marble, and almost as smooth. It had a beautiful shape, rising from a small foot to a full rounded body, with two curved handles, and tapering into a very narrow sealed neck. The jar alone must have accounted for a good part of the cost.

I hoped no one was watching, but Jesus must have seen me, for as I approached his chair he turned round to face me. He sat there, before me, his head at the level of my heart. His eyes were lifted with a look of expectation and humility, as though he knew what I was going to do. Around us the murmur of conversation continued.

I lifted the vase and he bowed his head in readiness. Suddenly I wondered how I was going to get the ointment out. How could I remove the seal? I panicked, for there was no time to lose. I took the neck between my two hands and snapped it off with a sudden, violent action. The crack echoed through the room. Everyone instantly fell silent. There was no question of holding back any ointment now – everything was his. The creamy unguent poured out – over my hands, over Jesus' hair, down his face and over his clothes. The lavish smell hit me like a flash of fire.

I stood there stupidly and stared at what I had done, drenched in an overpowering fragrance that dulled my other senses. What I saw and heard and felt all came to me as though through a screen, while it was the smell – the *smell* – that was closer to me than my own breath. It cocooned me. It burned my lungs. I drowned in it.

I looked at what was in my left hand, and in my right. I saw jagged stone needles, poking through the smooth rich cream. I looked at the head that was by my heart. I saw richly oiled hair, through which the silvery sludge was still slipping. I wanted to run my hands through his locks, but I was still holding the jagged vase. I knelt down to put it on the floor, and Jesus caught me there, by the shoulders. His face said thank you, thank you. Oh no, I wanted to reply, it is for me to thank you, and the thought overpowered me so that I wept. The tears flowed down my cheeks as though to wash away all my fear and all my shame, all my sin and all my foolishness.

It was now not Jesus' hair but his feet that I grasped, slipping them out of his sandals. And then I remembered the story of how his own cousin, John the Baptist, had once said he was unworthy to kneel down and undo the strap of his sandals. And that made me weep the more, for unthinkingly I had dared to do just that. I felt even more unworthy and sinful, and even more grateful that Jesus accepted me. I kissed his feet with love and gratitude and begging, and my tears ran over them so fast that I pulled my hair round my face to wipe away the wetness. The pound of oily ointment was now dripping down all round us, so I gathered handfuls of the stuff and rubbed it into his feet. And so I kissed and washed and dried and massaged his feet, until they were the most beautiful feet that ever could be imagined, feet fit for the most precious and vulnerable of all actions, that of walking to the scaffold.

SAINT JOHN

THE PASSION OF CHRIST

VERSION FROM THE *KING JAMES' BIBLE*

CHAPTER 18

When Jesus had spoken these words, he went forth with his disciples over the brook Cedron, where was a garden, into the which he entered, and his disciples.

And Judas also, which betrayed him, knew the place: for Jesus ofttimes resorted thither with his disciples.

Judas then, having received a band of men and officers from the chief priests and Pharisees, cometh thither with lanterns and torches and weapons.

Jesus therefore, knowing all things that should come upon him, went forth, and said unto them, Whom seek ye?

They answered him, Jesus of Nazareth. Jesus saith unto them, I am he. And Judas also, which betrayed him, stood with them.

As soon then as he had said unto them, I am he, they went backward, and fell to the ground.

Then asked he them again, Whom seek ye? And they said, Jesus of Nazareth.

Jesus answered, I have told you that I am he: if therefore ye seek me, let these go their way:

That the saying might be fulfilled, which he spake, 'Of them which thou gavest me have I lost none.

Then Simon Peter having a sword drew it, and smote the high priest's servant, and cut off his right ear. The servant's name was Malchus.

Then said Jesus unto Peter, Put up thy sword into the sheath: the cup which my Father hath given me, shall I not drink it?

Then the band and the captain and officers of the Jews took Jesus, and bound him,

And led him away to Annas first; for he was father in law to Caiaphas, which was the high priest that same year.

Now Caiaphas was he, which gave counsel to the Jews, that it was expedient that one man should die for the people.

And Simon Peter followed Jesus, and so did another disciple: that disciple was known unto the high priest, and went in with Jesus into the palace of the high priest.

But Peter stood at the door without. Then went out that other disciple, which was known unto the high priest, and spake unto her that kept the door, and brought in Peter.

Then saith the damsel that kept the door unto Peter, Art not thou also one of this man's disciples? He saith, I am not.

And the servants and officers stood there, who had made a fire of coals; for it was cold: and they warmed themselves: and Peter stood with them, and warmed himself.

The high priest then asked Jesus of his disciples, and of his doctrine.

Jesus answered him, I spake openly to the world: I ever taught, in the synagogue, and in the temple, whither the Jews always resort;

and in secret have I said nothing.

Why asketh thou me? ask them which heard me, what I have said unto them: behold, they know what I said.

And when he had thus spoken, one of the officers which stood by struck Jesus with the palm of his hand, saying, Answerest thou the high priest so?

Jesus answered him, If I have spoken evil, bear witness of the evil: but if well, why smitest thou me?

Now Annas had sent him bound unto Caiaphas the high priest.

And Simon Peter stood and warmed himself. They said therefore unto him, Art not thou also one of his disciples? He denied it, and said, I am not.

One of the servants of the high priest, being his kinsman whose ear Peter cut off, saith, Did not I see thee in the garden with him?

Peter then denied again: and immediately the cock crew.

Then led they Jesus from Caiaphas unto the hall of judgment: and it was early; and they themselves went not into the judgment hall, lest they should be defiled; but that they might eat the passover.

Pilate then went out unto them, and said. What accusation bring ye against this man?

They answered and said unto him, If he were not a malefactor, we would not have delivered him up unto thee.

Then said Pilate unto them, Take ye him, and judge him according to your law. The Jews therefore said unto him, It is not lawful for us to put any man to death:

That the saying of Jesus might be fulfilled, which he spake, signifying what death, he should die.

Then Pilate entered into the judgment hall again, and called Jesus, and said unto him, Art thou the King of the Jews?

Jesus answered him, Sayeth thou this thing of thyself, or did others tell it thee of me?

Pilate answered, Am I a Jew? Thine own nation and the chief priests have delivered thee unto me: what hast thou done?

Jesus answered, My kingdom is not of this world: if my kingdom were of this world, then would my servants fight, that I should not be delivered to the Jews: but now is my kingdom not from hence.

Pilate there said unto him, Art thou a king then? Jesus answered. Thou sayest that I am a king. To this end was I born, and for the cause came I into the world, that I should bear witness unto the truth. Every one that is of the truth heareth my voice.

Pilate saith unto him, What is truth? And when he had said this, he went out again unto the Jews, and saith unto them, I find in him no fault at all.

But ye have a custom, that I should release unto you one at the passover: will ye therefore that I release unto you the King of the Jews?

Then cried they all again, saying, Not this man, but Barabbas. Now Barabbas was a robber.

CHAPTER 19

Then Pilate therefore took Jesus, and scourged him.

And the soldiers plaited a crown of thorns, and put *it* on his head, and they put on him a purple robe.

And said, Hail, King of the Jews! and they smote him with their hands.

Pilate therefore went forth again, and saith unto them, Behold, I bring him forth to you, that ye may know that I find no fault in him.

Then came Jesus forth, wearing the crown of thorns, and the purple robe. And Pilate saith unto them, Behold the man!

When the chief priests therefore and officers saw him, they cried out, saying, Crucify him, crucify him. Pilate saith unto them, Take ye him, and crucify him: for I find no fault in him.

The Jews answered him, We have a law, and by our law he ought to die, because he made himself the Son of God.

When Pilate therefore heard that saying, he was the more afraid;

And went again into the judgment hall, and saith unto Jesus, Whence art thou? But Jesus gave him no answer.

Then saith Pilate unto him, Speakest thou not unto me? knowest thou not that I have power to crucify thee, and have power to release thee?

Jesus answered, Thou couldest have no power at all against me, except it were given thee from above: therefore he that delivered me unto thee hath the greater sin.

And from thenceforth Pilate sought to release him: but the Jews cried out, saying, If thou let this man go, thou art not Cæsar's friend: whosoever maketh himself a king speaketh against Cæsar.

When Pilate therefore heard that saying he brought Jesus forth, and sat down in the judgment seat in a place that is called the

Pavement, but in the Hebrew, Gabbatha.

And it was the preparation of the passover, and about the sixth hour: and he saith unto the Jews, Behold your King!

But they cried out, Away with him, away with him, crucify him. Pilate saith unto them, Shall I crucify your King? The chief priests answered, We have no king But Cæsar.

Then delivered he him therefore unto them to be crucified. And they took Jesus, and let him away.

And he bearing his cross went forth into a place called the place of a skull, which is called in the Hebrew Golgotha:

Where they crucified him, and two others with him, on either side one, and Jesus in the midst.

And Pilate wrote a title, and put it on the cross. And the writing was, Jesus of Nazareth the King of the Jews.

This title then read many of the Jews: for the place where Jesus was crucified was nigh to the city: and it was written in Hebrew, and Greek, and Latin.

Then said the chief priests of the Jews to Pilate, Write not, The King of the Jews: but that he said, I am King of the Jews.

Pilate answered, What I have written I have written.

Then the soldiers, when they had crucified Jesus, took his garments, and made four parts, to every soldier a part; and also his coat: now the coat was without seam, woven from the top throughout.

They said therefore among themselves, Let us not rend it, but cast losts for it, whose it shall be: that the scripture might be fulfilled, which saith, They parted my raiment among them, and for my vesture they did cast lots. These things therefore the soldiers did.

Now there stood by the cross of Jesus his mother, and his mother's sister, Mary the wife of Cleophas, and Mary Magdalene.

When Jesus therefore saw his mother, and the disciple standing by, whom he loved, he saith unto his mother, Woman, behold thy son!

Then saith he to the disciple, Behold thy mother! And from that hour that disciple took her unto his own home.

After this, Jesus knowing that all things were not accomplished, that the scripture might be fulfilled, saith, I thirst.

Now there was set a vessel full of vinegar: and they filled a sponge with vinegar, and put it upon hyssop, and put it to his mouth.

When Jesus therefore had received the vinegar, he said, It is finished: and he bowed his head, and gave up the ghost.

The Jews therefore, because it was the preparation, that the bodies should not remain upon the cross on the sabbath day, (for that sabbath day was an high day,) besought Pilate that their legs might be broken, and that they might be taken away.

Then came the soldiers, and brake the legs of the first, and of the other which was crucified with him.

But when they came to Jesus, and saw that he was dead already, they brake not his legs:

But one of the soldiers with a spear pierced his side, and forthwith came there out blood and water.

And he that saw it bare record, and his record is true; and he knoweth that he saith true, that ye might believe.

For these things were done, that the scripture should be fulfilled, A bone of him shall not be broken.

And again another scripture saith, They shall look on him whom they pierced.

And after this Joseph of Arimathæa, being a disciple of Jesus, but secretly for fear of the Jews, besought Pilate that he might take away the body of Jesus: and Pilate gave *him* leave. He came therefore, and took the body of Jesus.

And there came also Nicodemus, which at the first came to Jesus by night, and brought a mixture of myrrh and aloes, about an hundred pound weight.

Then took they the body of Jesus, and wound it in linen clothes with the spices, as the manner of the Jews is to bury.

Now in the place where he was crucified there was a garden; and in the garden a new sepulchre, wherein was never man yet laid.

There laid they Jesus therefore because of the Jews' preparation *day*: for the sepulchre was nigh at hand.

CYNEWULF (ATTRIB.)

From THE DREAM OF THE ROOD

Pause with me while I tell the most precious, the best
of dreams, sent to me in the deep silence of night
when men, word mongers, were everywhere at rest.

It seemed that I saw the most marvellous tree
lifted high on the air, and all haloed in light,
most beautiful of all beams of wood; a beacon

bathed in gold; there were breathtaking gems that stood
all around the base, a further five were ablaze
high along the cross-beam. Holy angels of the Lord

looked always on its loveliness, enthralled.
This was no criminal's cross; there came to gaze
the saintliest of spirits, men everywhere and all

marvels of creation mused upon it, where it stood.
How strange that tree of victory! and I – steeped in sin,
badly blemished all over – watched that glorious wood

adorned with banners, shining in all its beauty,
garlanded in gold, glorious gems worked in –
the wonderfully wreathed tree of the World's Ruler.

Yet straight through all that gold I could still see
the friend of once-wretched men, how it first began
to bleed on the right-hand side. Sorrow bore in on me,

and fear, before that vision; I saw the beacon change,
become clothed in colours; how at times the blood ran
drenching it in blood-dew, then how it bloomed with a strange

beauty. I lay a long while, wretched at heart,
watching my Saviour's tree; until suddenly most
wonderfully, the wood spoke, uttering these words:

'Long ago – distinctly I remember it! – one day
I was hewn down at the dark edge of the forest
and severed from my stem. Strong enemies seized me,

wrought me into a spectacle for the world to see,
commanding me to hoist their criminals on high;
men carried me on their shoulders and erected me

high on a hill – fixed there by many foes. I saw
the Ruler of mankind rush with real courage to climb
on me and I did not dare (my Lord had warned!)

bend down or break, though I saw the broad
surface of earth shiver; how simple – the Lord knows –
to smite his enemies! but firm and stout I stood,

unmoving. The hero stripped, though he was God Almighty!
robust and resolute, mounting onto the gallows
spirited, in the sight of many, to redeem mankind.

I wavered while the warrior embraced me: clasped me
and I did not dare bend down towards the ground,
fall on the earth's surface, I must stand fast.

I was raised up a rood, carrying the powerful King,
high Lord of Heaven, and did not dare to bend.
They pierced me with bloody nails, the pain still stings!

the open wounds of malice; they made us fools
together; I was wholly wet with blood
streaming from his side when he gave up his soul

and helpless on that hill I knew a fearful fate :
stretched out in agony the Almighty God
of hosts cruelly wracked; the heavens all in spate

above the body of our Ruler, that bright radiance;
shadows reigned supreme under a thickening cloud;
all of creation mourned, moaned this cruel chance:
and Christ was on the rood.'

TRANSLATION: JOHN F. DEANE

SAINT LUKE

THE EMPTY TOMB

VERSION FROM THE *KING JAMES' BIBLE*

Now upon the first day of the week, very early in the morning, they came unto the sepulchre, bringing the spices which they had prepared, and certain others with them.

And they found the stone rolled away from the sepulchre.

And they entered in, and found not the body of the Lord Jesus.

And it came to pass, as they were much perplexed thereabout, behold, two men stood by them in shining garments:

And as they were afraid, and bowed down their faces to the earth, they said unto them, Why seek ye the living among the dead?

He is not here, but is risen: remember how he spake unto you when he was yet in Galilee,

Saying, The Son of man must be delivered into the hands of sinful men, and be crucified, and the third day rise again.

And they remembered his words,

And returned from the sepulchre, and told all these things unto the eleven, and to all the rest.

It was Mary Magdalene, and Joanna, and Mary the mother of James, and other women that were with them, which told these things unto the apostles.

And their words seemed to them as idle tales, and they believed them not.

Then arose Peter, and ran unto the sepulchre; and stooping down, he beheld the linen clothes laid by themselves, and departed, wondering in himself at that which was come to pass.

And, behold, two of them went that same day to a village called Emmaus, which was from Jerusalem about threescore furlongs.

And they talked together of all these things which had happened.

And it came to pass, that, while they communed together and reasoned, Jesus himself drew near, and went with them.

But their eyes were holden that they should not know him.

And he said unto them, What manner of communications are these that ye have one to another, as ye walk, and are sad?

And the one of them, whose name was Cleopas, answering said

unto him, Art thou only a stranger in Jerusalem, and hast not known the things which are come to pass there in these days?

And he said unto them, What things? And they said unto him, Concerning Jesus of Nazareth, which was a prophet mighty in deed and word before God and all the people:

And how the chief priests and our rulers delivered him to be condemned to death, and have crucified him.

But we trusted that it had been he which should have redeemed Israel: and beside all this, today is the third day since these things were done.

Yea, and certain women also of our company made us astonished, which were early at the sepulchre;

And when they found not his body, they came, saying, that they had also seen a vision of angels, which said that he was alive.

And certain of them which were with us went to the sepulchre, and found it even so as the women had said: but him they saw not.

Then he said unto them, O fools, and slow of heart to believe all that the prophets have spoken:

Ought not Christ to have suffered these things, and to enter into his glory?

And beginning at Moses and all the prophets, he expounded unto them in all the scriptures the things concerning himself.

And they drew nigh unto the village, whither they went: and he made as though he would have gone further.

But they constrained him, saying, Abide with us: for it is toward evening, and the day is far spent. And he went in to tarry with them.

And it came to pass, as he sat at meat with them, he took bread, and blessed it, and brake, and gave to them,

And their eyes were opened, and they knew him; and he vanished out of their sight.

And they said one to another, Did not our heart burn within us, while he talked with us by the way, and while he opened to us the scriptures?

And they rose up the same hour, and returned to Jerusalem and found the eleven gathered together, and them that were with them,

Saying, The Lord is risen indeed, and hath appeared to Simon.

And they told what things were done in the way, and how he was known of them in breaking of bread.

And as they thus spake, Jesus himself stood in the midst of them, and saith unto them, Peace be unto you,

But they were terrified and affrighted, and supposed that they had seen a spirit.

And he said unto them, Why are ye troubled? and why do thoughts arise in your hearts?

Behold my hands and my feet, that it is I myself: handle me, and see; for a spirit hath not flesh and bones, as ye see me have.

And when he had thus spoken, he shewed them his hands and his feet.

And while they yet believed not for joy, and wondered, he said unto them, Have ye here any meat?

And they gave him a piece of broiled fish, and of an honeycomb.

And he took it, and did eat before them.

And he said unto them, These are the words which I spake unto you, while I was yet with you, that all things must be fulfilled, which were written in the law of Moses, and in the prophets, and in the psalms, concerning me.

Then opened he their understanding, that they might understand the scriptures.

And said unto them, Thus it is written, and thus it behoved Christ to suffer, and to rise from the dead the third day:

And that repentance and remission of sins should be preached in his name among all nations, beginning at Jerusalem.

And ye are witnesses of these things.

And, behold, I send the promise of my Father upon you: but tarry ye in the city of Jerusalem, until ye be endowed with power from on high.

And he led them out as far as to Bethany, and he lifted up his hands, and blessed them.

And it came to pass, while he blessed them, he was parted from them, and carried up into heaven.

And they worshipped him, and returned to Jerusalem with great joy:

And were continually in the temple, praising and blessing God. Amen.

THE FOREST OF THE DEAD

G. K. CHESTERTON

THE DEATH OF SAINT FRANCIS

There is something profoundly pathetic, and full of great problems, in the fact that at last, as it would seem, his flame of life leapt up and his heart rejoiced when they saw afar off on the Assisian hills the solemn pillars of the Portiuncula. He who had become a vagabond for the sake of a vision, he who had denied himself all sense of place and possession, he whose whole gospel and glory it was to be homeless, received like a Parthian shot from nature, the sting of the sense of home. He also had his *maladie du clocher*, his sickness of the spire; though his spire was higher than ours. 'Never,' he cried, with the sudden energy of strong spirits in death, 'Never give up this place. If you would go anywhere or make any pilgrimage return always to your home, for this is the holy house of God.' . . .

After he had taken farewell of some of his nearest, and especially some of his oldest, friends he was lifted at his own request off his own rude bed and laid on the bare ground, as some say clad only in a hair shirt as he had first gone forth into the wintry woods from the presence of his father. It was the final assertion of his great fixed idea; of praise and thanks springing to their most towering heights out of wickedness and nothing. As he lay there we may be certain that his teared and blinded eyes saw nothing but their object and origin. We may be sure that the soul in its last inconceivable isolation, was face to face with nothing less than God Incarnate and Christ Crucified. But for the men standing around him there must have been other thoughts mingling with these, and many memories must have gathered like ghosts in the twilight, as that day wore on and that great darkness descended in which we all lost a friend . . . Round about him stood the brethren in their brown habits, those that had loved him even if they afterwards disputed with each other . . . A man might fancy that the birds must have known when it happened and made some motion in the evening sky. As they had once, according to the tale, scattered to the four winds of heaven in the pattern of a cross at his signal of dispersion; they might now have written in such dotted lines, a more awful augury across the sky.

Hidden in the woods perhaps were little crawling creatures never again to be so much noticed and understood, and it has been said that animals are sometimes conscious of things to which man their spiritual superior is for the moment blind. We do not know whether any shiver passed through all the thieves and the outcasts and the outlaws, to tell them what had happened to him who never knew the nature of scorn. But at least in the passages and porches of the Portiuncula there was a sudden stillness when all the brown figures stood like little bronze statues, for the stopping of the great heart that had not broken till it held the world.

EMILY DICKINSON

OUR JOURNEY HAD ADVANCED

Our journey had advanced,
Our feet were almost come
To that odd fork in being's road,
Eternity by term.

Our pace took sudden awe,
Our feet reluctant led;
Before were cities, but between,
The forest of the dead.

Retreat was out of hope;
Behind, a sealed route,
Eternity's white flag before,
And God at every gate.

WILLIAM SHAKESPEARE

FEAR NO MORE THE HEAT O' THE SUN

Fear no more the heat o' the sun,
　　Nor the furious winter's rages;
Thou thy worldly task hast done,
　　Home art gone, and ta'en thy wages;
Golden lads and girls all must
As chimney-sweepers, come to dust.

Fear no more the frown o' the great,
　　Thou art past the tyrant's stroke:
Care no more to clothe and eat;
　　To thee the reed is as the oak;
The sceptre, learning, physic, must
All follow this, and come to dust.

Fear no more the lightning-flash,
　　Nor the all-dreaded thunder-stone;
Fear not slander, censure rash;
　　Thou hast finish'd joy and moan:
All lovers young, all lovers must
　　Consign to thee, and come to dust.

No exorciser harm thee!
　　Nor no witchcraft charm thee!
Ghost unlaid forbear thee!
　　Nothing ill come near thee!
Quiet consummation have;
　　And renowned be thy grave!

EMILY DICKINSON

THIS WORLD IS NOT CONCLUSION

This World is not Conclusion.
A Species stands beyond –
Invisible, as Music –
But positive, as Sound –
It beckons, and it baffles –
Philosophy – don't know –
And through a Riddle, at the last –
Sagacity, must go –
To guess it, puzzles scholars –
To gain it, Men have borne
Contempt of Generations
And Crucifixion, shown –
Faith slips – and laughs, and rallies –
Blushes, if any see –
Plucks at a twig of Evidence –
And asks a Vane, the way –
Much Gesture, from the Pulpit –
Strong Hallelujahs roll –
Narcotics cannot still the Tooth
That nibbles at the soul –

JULIAN OF NORWICH

AND ALL SHALL BE WELL

After this the Lord brought to my mind the longing that I had to Him afore. And I saw that nothing letted me but sin. And so I looked, generally, upon us all, and methought: *If sin had not been, we should all have been clean and like to our Lord, as He made us.*

And thus, in my folly, afore this time often I wondered why by the great foreseeing wisdom of God the beginning of sin was not letted: for then, methought, all should have been well. This stirring [of mind] was much to be forsaken, but nevertheless mourning and sorrow I made therefor, without reason and discretion.

But Jesus, who in this Vision informed me of all that is needful to me, answered by this word and said: *It behoved that there should be sin; but all shall be well, and all shall be well, and all manner of thing shall be well.*

In this naked word *sin*, our Lord brought to my mind, generally, *all that is not good*, and the shameful despite and the utter noughting that He bare for us in this life, and His dying; and all the pains and passions of all His creatures, ghostly and bodily; (for we be all partly noughted, and we shall be noughted following our Master, Jesus, till we be full purged, that is to say, till we be fully noughted of our deadly flesh and of all our inward affections which are not very good;) and the beholding of this, with all pains that ever were or ever shall be, - and with all these I understand the Passion of Christ for most pain, and overpassing. All this was shewed in a touch and quickly passed over into comfort: for our good Lord would not that the soul were affeared of this terrible sight.

But I saw not *sin*: for I believe it hath no manner of substance nor no part of being, nor could it be known but by the pain it is cause of.

And thus pain, *it* is something, as to my sight, for a time; for it purgeth, and maketh us to know ourselves and to ask mercy. For the Passion of our Lord is comfort to us against all this, and so is His blessed will. And for the tender love that our good Lord hath to all that shall be saved, He comforteth readily and sweetly, signifying thus: *It is sooth that sin is cause of all this pain; but all shall be well, and all shall be well, and all manner [of] thing shall be well.*

These words were said full tenderly, showing no manner of blame to me nor to any that shall be saved. Then were it a great unkindness to blame or wonder on God for my sin, since He blameth not me for sin.

And in these words I saw a marvellous high mystery hid in God, which mystery He shall openly make known to us in Heaven: in which knowing we shall verily see the cause why He suffered sin to come. In which sight we shall endlessly joy in our Lord God.

BIOGRAPHICAL NOTES

W. H. AUDEN (1907-1973) was one of the twentieth century's leading poets. While he became famous as a Thirties poet whose themes included socialism and love, much of his later work is deeply Christian. His many books included *Poems* (1928), *The Dyer's Hand* (essays, 1962) and *The Shield of Achilles* (poems, 1955).

ST AUGUSTINE (354-430) is the author of *Confessions*, an account of his own religious journey from Christianity to Manichaenism and back to Christianity. The struggles faced in his search have struck a chord of truth with many readers over the centuries. In 396, he became bishop of Hippo. His other works include *De Civitate Dei* (413-427). He is something of a bugbear for certain contemporary thinkers, most notably for the main proponent of 'creation spirituality', Mathew Fox.

RICHARD BAXTER (1615-1691) was an English military chaplain. His books include *Call to the Unconverted* (1657) and *The Saint's Everlasting Rest* (1650). He also wrote hymns.

THE VENERABLE BEDE (673-735) was a historian whose greatest work was *Historia Ecclesiastica Gentis Anglorum* (731), an ecclesiastical histroy of the English People. He also wrote on science and produced a number of biblical commentaries. He spent most of his life at Jarrow.

GEORGE BERNANOS (1888-1948) was a French writer whose Catholicism permeated his finest books. His best-known book, *Journal d'un Curé de Campagne* (*Diary of a Country Priest*), was published in 1936.

SIR JOHN BETJEMAN (1906-1984) was a poet whose work, to some, is unbearably light and, to others, delightfully immediate. Unlike many minor poets, he created a poetic world that was completely his own. The Church of England is an important part of that nostalgic world. His writings on architecture are among his finest work.

WILLIAM BLAKE (1757-1827) was a visionary poet whose work cannot be fully understood without taking its religious and mystical elements into account. He was also an engraver. His books included *Songs of Innocence* (1789) and *Poetical Sketches* (1783). Many of his contemporaries considered him quite mad, though countless readers now find him eminently sane. His poems range from simple lyrics to large, mythological works.

LEONARDO BOFF (born 1938) is a Brazilian Franciscan and liberation theologian. He was educated in Brazil and in the great universities of Europe. His best-known work, *Jesus-Christ Librator* (1972) offers hope and justice for the oppressed. He has also written widely on other subjects, including the reform of church structures.

EAVAN BOLAND (born 1944) is one of Ireland's leading contemporary poets. Her poetry and criticism display the workings of a brilliant and restless intelligence upon themes and forms. Her concerns include the place of women writers, history, suburban life, Dublin, art. Her collections include *The Journey* (1987), *Selected Poems* (1989) and *In a Time of Violence* (1994).

DIETRICH BONHOEFFER (1906-1945) was a theologian and pastor involved in the Confessing Church, part of an anti-Hitler movement in Germany. He was involved with plans to kill Hitler and was imprisoned in 1943. He was hanged in Flossenburg prison two years later. His letters from prison combine to form a powerful example of Christian thinking at the heart of the modern world. His writings can be found in a number of books, including *Ethics* (English edition 1955) and *Letters and Papers from Prison* (SCM Press, 1971).

ROY CAMPBELL (1901-57) was born in Natal but spent much of his life in England and Europe. In 1935 he became a Catholic and fought for Franco in Spain. He published many translations from French and Spanish.

WILLIAM CARELTON (1794-1869) was the author of *Traits and Stories of the Irish Peasantry* (1830-1835) and *Black Prophet* (1847). His work was to influence many later writers, among them Patrick Kavanagh and Benedict Kiely (who wrote a biography of Carleton). His account of Lough Derg is worth comparing with the work of Kavanagh, Seamus Heaney and Denis Devlin, all of whom set major poems in this famous place of pilgrimage.

ST CATHERINE OF SIENNA (1347-1380) corresponded with a wide circle of friends, popes among them. She was a Dominican nun whose renowned talent for diplomacy was made use of in a number of major contemporary disputes. Her feast falls on 30 April.

G. K. CHESTERTON (1874-1936) was on of the most famous journalists of his day. He also wrote novels, poems and detective stories - the latter featuring Fr Brown. Chesterton converted to Catholicism in 1922. He wrote widely on religious themes and his books include *Orthodoxy* (1909) and *Heretics* (1905). The journalist in him used the attraction of the ephemeral to prove the worth of the eternal; ultimately, this militated against the endurance of his work.

ST CLARE OF ASSISI (1194-1253) founded the Order of the Poor Clares. She is associated with St Francis of Assisi (her 'spiritual brother') but is best seen in her own right as a strong-minded woman for whom the Franciscan spirit was a gift that she developed into her own particular charism. Her contemplative order is now found worldwide.

CYNEWULF probably lived in the 9th century and is said to be the author of 'The Dream of The Road', among other poems. Many scholars dispute this. Whatever the case, the poem itself is one of the great Old English works. Another of his poems concerns the connection between St Helena and the True Cross, a subject which also became a theme for Evelyn Waugh in his novel *Helena*, an excerpt from which is included in this anthology.

KING DAVID is held to be the author of the *Psalms*, a collection of songs which make for one of the glories of the Old Testament. For centuries, the Psalms have been part of the daily recital of the Office in religious orders. Whether they are chanted or read, familiarity with them offers what Thomas Merton termed a tabernacle of words.

DOROTHY DAY (1897-1980) was the co-founder of the Catholic Worker Movement in America. She was an uncompromising believer in the importance of social justice and was jailed a number of times. She wrote many articles for *The Catholic Worker*. Her books include *From Union Square to Rome* (1938) and *The Long Loneliness* (1952).

JOHN F. DEANE (born 1943) is a poet, fiction writer and publisher. He runs the Dedalus Press in Dublin, a house which publishes work by poets from Ireland and many other countries. Many of his own poems are informed by a deep spirituality. His books include *The Stylized City, Road with Cypress and Star,* and *Winter in Meath.*

EMILY DICKINSON (1830-1886) was born in Amherst, Massachusetts. With Walt Whitman, she is the leading Amercian poet of the nineteenth century. Where Whitman's work is expansive, public and crowded. Emily Dickinson's is enclosed, private and intense. Most of her poems were published for the first time after her death.

JOHN DONNE (1572-1631) was born into a Catholic family but later renounced

Catholicism, and ended by becoming (on the advice of King James I) an Anglican chaplain. Famous as a poet and preacher, his work ranges from great love poems to religious sonnets. His life was marked by personal tragedy and a sharp sense of survival.

MEISTER ECKHART (1260-1327) was a Dominican priest and mystic whose opinions rankled with many Church officials but who is now seen by many as a major religious figure. His writing is accessible without being simplistic, and his use of clear images and statements leaves a clear mark on the memory.

GEORGE ELIOT (Mary Ann Evans) (1819-1880) was a novelist and translator whose works included *Middlemarch* (1871-1872), *Daniel Deronda* (1874-1876), *Adam Bede* (1859) and *Silas Marner* (1861). Her translations included Strauss's *Life of Jesus* (1846) and Feuerbach's *Essence of Christianity* (1854).

PADRAIC FALLON (1905-1974) was a leading Irish poet. His first collection appeared in the same year as his death. *The Collected Poems* appeared in 1980 (Gallery/Carcanet).

ST FRANCIS OF ASSISI (1181-1226) was a poet and founder of the Franciscan order. His spirituality was rooted in a love for poverty and for the natural world. The simplicity and humility of his outlook is even more startling and challenging today.

LADY AUGUSTA GREGORY (1852-1932) lived a Coole Park in County Galway after she married Sir William Gregory in 1880. She was a close friend of W. B. Yeats and was closely involved with the development of the Abbey Theatre. She was a playwright and folklore collector whose books include *Poets and Dreamers* (1903) and *Gods and Fighting Men* (1904).

MARGARET HEBBLETHWAITE (born 1951) is a writer and journalist whose books include *Motherhood and God* (1984), *Basic is Beautiful* (1993) and *Six New Gospels; New Testament Women Tell Their Stories* (1994). She works with the Catholic weekly paper, *The Tablet*.

PETER HEBBLETHWAITE (1930-1994) was the leading Catholic journalist of his time in England. His books included biographies of Pope John XXIII and Pope Paul VI. He was an expert on the machinations of the Vatican, and his outspokenness was one of the best features of his journalism.

HILDEGARD OF BINGEN (1098-1179) was a German mystic, writer and composer who was believed to have prophetic gifts. She is one of a number of women mystics whose lives and work have taken on new importance in recent years. Her hymns have been recorded by the Irish singer Noirin Ní Riain, among others.

GEORGE HERBERT (1593-1633) was a poet and clergyman. His poems are among the finest religious literature in English. He explained to a friend that his poems are 'a picture of the many spiritual conflicts that have passed betwixt God and my soul, before I could subject mine to the will of Jesus my Master'.

GERARD MANLEY HOPKINS (1844-1889) was a poet and Jesuit priest whose religious tussles and crises found a correlative in poems that were equally complex with regard to language and rhythm. He was also a great nature poet. Under the influence of Cardinal Newman's conversion, he became a Catholic in !886. His reputation was almost non-existent in his lifetime but it is now secure.

ST JOHN was on of the four authors of the New Testament gospels. For many people, his gospel is the most powerful of the four. It shows Christ wth great intimacy and also tells more about his life in the urban world of Jerusalem.

ST JOHN OF THE CROSS (1542-1592) was a Spanish poet, mystic and Caremlite friar. In 1577, he was imprisoned as a result of his views. The experience of prison proved to be pivotal. Unlike many poets who deal with religion as a subject, John of the Cross is a very great writer indeed. His other works are accounts of the mystical life and are written with an exactitude and precision that might equally characterise works of science. His works include *The Spiritual Canticle* and *The Dark Night*. He was a close friend of Saint Teresa of Avila.

JULIAN OF NORWICH (c.1342-1416) was an English mystic and anchoress who lived for many years in a cell in Norwich. She experienced a number of visions, which she described in *Revelations of Divine Love*. Her writing has a wonderful immediacy about it that manages to communicate religious feeling in a tactile and intimate manner.

MARY LOUDON (born 1966) is a poet, journalist and writer whose books include series of interviews with nuns and Anglican ministers. She writes for many British newspapers, among them *The Independent*, the *Daily Mail* and the *Sunday Telegraph*.

ST LUKE, who wrote one of the four gospels, was a doctor— a factor reflected in the number of his stories that deal with the ability of Jesus to heal the sick. Like Jesus himself, Luke seems to have had a particular affinity with women.

PATRICK KAVANAGH (1905-1967) was a poet, journalist and novelist. He is Ireland's best-loved modern poet and, as Anthony Cronin once pointed out, Kavanagh's poems have entered the public mind in a manner similar to the way in which the work of Robert Burns is part of the Scottish consciousness. Kavanagh was a deeply religious man whose faith is relflected in many of his poems.

PHILIP LARKIN (1922-1985) was an English poet and novelist. He worked for many years as a librarian and also wrote on jazz. He published four volumes of poems and a *Collected Poems* was published by Faber and Faber after his death.

CATHERINE PHIL MacCARTHY (born 1954) is a poet and drama teacher. Born in County Limerick, she now lives in Dublin. Her first collection of poems, *At This Hour of the Tide*, was published by Salmon Poetry in 1994.

JOHN McGAHERN (born 1935) is a novelist and short story writer. Many of his works are milestones in contemporary Irish fiction, most notably his novel *Amongst Women.* He is a superb stylist whose work is as well-honed as poetry, and for whom the images in a story are as important as the plot.

GEORGE MACKAY BROWN (born 1921) is the great modern poet of the Orkney Islands. His work reflects island history, folklore, people and nature. He is a Catholic whose poems, stories and novels often carry the influence of his faith.

ST MATHEW, one of the gospel-writers, worked as a tax collector until he decided to follow Christ. He describes miracles and parables, and also gives us the words of the Lord's Prayer.

MOTHER MARIBEL OF WANTAGE (1887-1970) was an Anglican nun. She was also an artist who had trained at the Slade.

THOMAS MERTON (1915-1968) was a poet, writer and Cistercian monk. His work has been hugely influential and he illustrates the paradox of how a contemplative can be at the core of contemporary issues and not hidden in a cocoon from which the modern world is excluded. His many books include *Seeds of Contemplation*, *Conjectures of a Guilty Bystander* and *The Collected Poems of Thomas Merton*.

JOHN HENRY NEWMAN (1801–1890) was a Catholic convert whose conversion became at once influential and controversial when it occured in 1845. He was ordained the following year and in 1879 he became a cardinal. He wrote of religion with an intellectual firmness that could still admit the elusiveness of faith. He spent many years in Ireland as rector of the Catholic University. His works include *Apologia Pro Vita Sua*, *The Dream of Gerontius* (a poem), and *The Idea of a University Defined and Illustrated*. His sermons have also been published. One of the greatest minds of his time, the resonances of Newman's position and thought continue to be experienced.

KATE O'BRIEN (1897–1974) was a novelist, travel-writer, biographer, journalist and translator. She was born in Limerick. Her books include *Without My Cloak*, *The Land of Spices*, *As Music and Splendour* and *Distingushed Villa*. Her biography of St Teresa of Avila treats of the saint as a woman of genius, in much the same way as another might treat of the genius of Picasso of Joyce. This approach frees her from hagiographical pitfalls.

BLAISE PASCAL (1623–1662) was a mathematician, scientist, inventor, writer and philosopher. His achievements included the invention of a crude calculating apparatus and the writing of the *Pensées*, a series of notes in defence of Christianity. Varying from the aphoristic to the essay-like, the *Pensées*, despite their unpolished form, teem with insight and startling ideas.

ST PATRICK (d. c. 493 AD) left Wales for Ireland in 432 AD. His grandfather had been a priest at a time before rules on celibacy applied. According to the *Annals of the Four Masters*, Bishop Patrick was sent by Pope Celestine to convert the Irish. He is Ireland's national saint and his feast-day falls on 17 March. His writings include *The Confession* and *Letter Against the Soldiers of Coroticus*.

DAPHNE D. C. POCHIN MOULD has lived in Ireland since the early 1950s and has produced a remarkably wide range of books and articles. She is a pilot and serial photographer, and she now lives in County Cork. Her books include *Ireland of the Saints*, *Irish Pilgrimage*, *The Monastries of Ireland* and *Discovering Cork*.

RICHARD ROLLE (c. 1300–1349) was a hermit and writer who was born in Yorkshire. His religious writings unite the experience of a mystic with a gift of simple and memorable expression. His most famous work is *The Fire of Love*.

JAMES ROOSE-EVANS is a non-stipendiary Anglican priest who has worked for many years in theatre. His books include an autobiography and a book on the contemporary use of rituals.

WILLIAM SHAKESPEARE (1564–1616) grew up in Stratford-Upon-Avon and later moved to London, where he worked with the Globe Theatre. Even a brief list of his plays is a litany of genius: *Hamlet, King Lear, Richard II, The Tempest*. His poems, whether sonnet, narrative or lyric, were just as magnificent.

KING SOLOMON was reowned for his wisdom and also for the scale of his ambition. Whether he is the author or the great protagonist of the 'Song of Songs' is impossible to say. The work is a remarkable love poem and was read at Passover by many Jews, who saw in its portrayal of an amorous relationship a metaphor for the relationship between God and the Chosen People. *The Song of Songs* has been translated by many writers, with a new version appearing in France as recently as 1993. The King James' version in English is probably impossible to surpass.

FRANCIS STUART (born 1902) is one of Ireland's leading novelists, though that phrase conveys little of the complexity that marks his life and work. He lived and worked in Nazi Germany. His books include *Redemption, A Pillar of Cloud, Memorial* and *Black List: Section H*. Less concerned with neatly finished forms than with a sense of disturbance and displacement, his work is often closer to the works of Simone Weil or Julian of Norwich than to more literary models (with the exception of Dostoievsky). One of his earliest works was a small pamphlet on mysticism.

ST TERESA OF AVILA (1515-1582) was a Carmelite and writer. She founded the Discalced Carmelites in 1562. Her works include an autobiography (most recently published as *The Life of Saint Teresa of Avila by Herself*), *The Way of Perfection, The Book of Foundations* and *The Interior Castle*. There is at once something very ordinary and extraordinary about her. As she wrote: '*Entre los pucheros anda el Senor*' – 'The Lord walks among the saucepans.'

ST THÉRÈSE OF LISIEUX (1873-1897) was a Carmelite nun whose life has been sentimentalised in a manner that fails to do her justice. She displayed a knowledge of God existing among the ordinary days of an ordinary life and, in this way, (to use a phrase of Eavan Boland's) she 'sanctified the common.' She suffered periods of intense religious doubt and also, in her final years, of severe physical pain. Her autobiography is a classic of spirituality.

R. S. THOMAS (born 1913) is a poet and retired clergyman. His work is marked by the presence of his native Wales and its country people, and by a strong religious element that marks him out from many contemporary poets. His plainness makes him closer to the tradition of George Herbert than to Hopkins, though the sense of struggle with religious ideas is something with which Hopkins would have been only too familiar.

HENRY DAVID THOREAU (1817-1862) was a writer and, as he described himself, 'mystic, a transcendalist, and a natural philosopher to boot'. His greatest work was *Walden, an account of his life in a hut near the edge of Walden Pond in Massachussetts.*

EVELYN UNDERHILL (1875-1941) was an Anglican poet, novelist, writer and theologian. Her works include *Mysticism, The Mystic Way* and *The Spiritual Life.*

HENRY VAUGHAN (1621-1695) was a poet whose finest work is profoundly religious. He was influenced by the work of George Herbert, but where Herbert's work exemplifies piety (in the best sense), Vaughan's is more mystical and cosmological.

JEAN VANIER (born 1928) is the founder of the l'Arche communities. L'Arche has offered a home to handicapped people in many parts of the world. For Vanier, the handicapped are people who can teach; they are not victims to be patronised.

SIMONE WEIL (1909-1942) was the greatest religious writer of the twentieth century. She worked as a teacher, farmhand and factory worker. She enlisted in the Republican forces during the Spanish civil war. Her mystical experiences fuelled her life, and while her work is often difficult, it typifies a thoroughness of thought that is seldom brought to bear on religious questions. Her works include *Waiting on God* (an essential text, from which both extracts in this anthology are taken), *Gravity and Grace,* and *The Need for Roots.* She died in London after a period during which she refused to eat more than those who suffered under Nazi occupation in France.

EVELYN WAUGH (1903-1966) was a novelist who became a Catholic in 1930. His scabrous personality covered an inner sense of disorder that, perhaps, was attracted to the fixity and firmness of Catholic dogma. He was appalled by the Second Vatican Council. His books include *A Handful of Dust, Vile Bodies, Brideshead Revisited* and *Helena.*

INDEX OF AUTHORS AND POETS